BIRDS EYE VIEW OF SAN DIEGO, SAN DIEGO BAY AND CORONADO BEACH — 1887

SAN DIEGO ORIGINALS
Profiles of the movers and shakers of California's first community

PANAMA-CALIFORNIA EXPOSITION SITE.

San Diego Originals

Profiles of the movers
and shakers of California's
first community

By Theodore W. Fuller

California Profiles Publications   Pleasant Hill, California

Cover design by Aleksander Kardas

Library of Congress Cataloging-in-Publication Data

Fuller, Theodore W.
　　San Diego originals .

　　Includes index.
　　1. San Diego (Calif.) — Biography. I. Title.
F869.S22F85 1987 920'.079498 87-71017
ISBN 0-943379-00-8
ISBN 0-943379-01-6 (pbk.)

Profiles of Lt. George H. Derby, Agoston Haraszthy and Jedediah Smith previously appeared in *PG&E Progress*, published by Pacific Gas & Electric Co. of San Francisco, and have been revised by the author.

Contents

Introduction

Ask a San Diegan what's so great about the city. Typically, the answer underscores the climate, the setting, the water, the healthy ambiance.

Some residents respond, "Why, it's the people who made this city what it is today."

This book blends both elements — the people and the place.

But the people dominate. The range in time includes Cabrillo's discovery of San Diego Bay on September 28, 1542 to the early years of World War II. The brief profiles reveal what attracted them, how they sought their goals, their reactions to success or failure and, whenever possible, what motivated them and who influenced them.

These people left an indelible imprint on the area. Some of them, like John Charles Frémont and Lieutenant George Horatio Derby, stayed but briefly. Colonel Ed Fletcher and tuna fishing industry skipper M. O. Medina spent most of their adult lives in San Diego. Not one of these originals can claim San Diego for a birthplace. Even the town dog, Bum, was an emigré from Los Angeles.

Natives take pride in being part of California's first community, but old-timers experienced feelings of inadequacy when Los Angeles or San Francisco outshone their city. Perhaps because of slow growth, the San Diego area suffered less from fools and scoundrels than cities to the north. Not that they didn't exist. Their shenanigans just lacked the impact of big league con men and crooks elsewhere.

San Diego lures included the promise of riches. Developers Alonzo Erastus Horton and William Heath Davis sought paydirt from the sale of building lots. George Marston and Ah Quin searched for manna from merchandise sold in their stores.

Wealth and health attracted Elisha Babcock, who dreamed up Coronado and its first hotel, and Frank Kimball, who was the prime mover in establishing National City.

The search for improved health and a mission of serving others brought Henry Restarick, the third rector to serve at St. Paul's Episcopal Church. Author Helen Hunt Jackson hoped her words would achieve justice and compassion for the Indians.

Another writer, William Smythe, aimed for nothing less than utopia, based on his knowledge of irrigation techniques and the need for people to socialize. Katherine Tingley based her utopian dream on theosophy and brotherhood.

Those utopian ideas fizzled, at least in the San Diego area. Many of today's residents and visitors, however, find San Diego, if not eactly utopia, still an ideal place in which to work, to play, to plan for tomorrow. It's a tomorrow filled with promise, thanks to many of the originals described in this book.

Acknowledgments

"**F**or our next series** why don't you write some short biographical sketches of California pioneers?"

This question, posed by Stan Turnbull late in 1979, led to twenty-seven "California Originals" in Pacific Gas & Electric Company's *PG&E Progress*, a monthly eight-page publication I wrote and edited at the time. It reaches 3.5 million Northern California customers every month along with their bills. The response indicated people from all walks of life enjoy finding out about the men and women who made an original impact on the state.

Turnbull, then head of the company's publication section, and Don J. Baxter, manager of our department, provided ideas and editing talents. PG&E kindly granted permission to use the sketches of George H. Derby, Agoston Haraszthy and Jedediah Smith, which appear in slightly longer versions in this work.

So thanks go to these two men, PG&E and to friends and helpers like Irma Somerton, librarian at Contra Costa County's Central Library in Pleasant Hill. She reviewed the manuscript in her spare time and gave helpful suggestions as did Jerry and Shary Hammon; George Emanuels, whose latest book is *The History of Contra Costa County*; Fran Lavin; Kristine Olsen Brasssil; Bob Little; Valerie Fulton and Patricia Edwards. Valerie and Pat are mainstays of the Alma Den Writers Club, a group of uninhibited, supportive people whose critiques proved valuable. Help and suggestions also came from Larry and Chris Menkin, Danny Daniels, Chuck Goodmacher, my daughter Elizabeth and my wife Betty, whose patience and encouragement smoothed many a wrinkle between idea and the printed page.

Staff members and volunteers at the San Diego Historical Society, the San Diego Public Library, the Bancroft Library on the University of California's Berkeley campus and the California State Library in Sacramento also deserve credit. Anyone who writes about San Diego ends up endebted to Richard F. Pourade, author of a six-volume series, *The History of San Diego*, published by The Union-Tribune Publishing Company, and to William E. Smythe, who wrote *History of San Diego*, published in 1908 by The History Company. Two favorite sources of concise and often colorful information about the state are *California: An Interpretive History* by Walton Bean and James J. Rawls, published by McGraw-Hill, Inc., and *California: An Illustrated History* by T. H. Watkins, published by American West Publishing Company. And to the biographers and other sources credited in the following profiles I am also grateful.

Theodore W. Fuller

Dedicated to my wife Betty Ann whose help, encouragement and sense of humor made this project easier, feasible and more fun.

Rugged regimen of seamen in the 1830s intrigued readers of Dana's Two Years Before the Mast. *A case of measles had strained his eyes so he signed up for a sea voyage at the age of l9 and graphically recorded California impressions.*

Richard Henry Dana:
Chaste observer of California

With his book *Two Years Before the Mast*, Richard Henry Dana, Jr. accomplished two things:
1. Seamen achieved better working conditions, thanks to Dana's vivid description of the regimen aboard the Pilgrim under a sometimes sadistic captain. 2. After the book came out in 1840, Americans gained a clearer picture of California people, conditions and customs, along with the area's potential.

One thing Dana did not accomplish nor even attempt: to heal the rift between his family and William Goodwin Dana, an uncle who had sailed from Boston in 1826 and settled near Santa Barbara. There William joined the Catholic Church and after two years of red tape became a Mexican citizen. These steps enabled him to wed Josefa Carrillo, the daughter of a prominent local family who was sixteen when they married, and acquire ownership of the property the Carrillos gave them.

William Dana, who became a successful merchant, isn't mentioned in *Two Years Before the Mast*. Richard didn't even look him up on the occasions when the *Pilgrim* anchored at Santa Barbara.

Richard Dana was "a proper Bostonian with an uncompromising puritan ethic," said Carol Dunlap in *California People*. His grandfather served as a Massachusetts Supreme Court chief justice and his father gained renown as a writer. So family pride, patriotism and decorum influenced the young sojourner. He had signed on as a seaman, hoping sea duty would improve his eyesight, which a case of measles had impaired. The problem halted his studies at Harvard University.

When the *Pilgrim* reached San Diego in 1835, the nineteen-year-old Dana noted: "Having a good breeze, we stood round the point, and hauling our wind, brought the little harbor, which is rather the outlet of a small river, right before us . . . A chain of high hills, beginning at the point . . . protected the harbor on the north and west, and ran off into the interior as far as the eye could reach. On the other side, the land was low, and green, but without trees."

Most of the residents had "California fever" — Dana's phrase for laziness. "The men are thriftless, proud and extravagant, and very much given to gaming; and the women have but little education, and a good deal of beauty, and their morality, of course is none of the best," Dana wrote.

As for the Mexicans' proclivity for revolutions, "Instead of caucusing, paragraphing, libelling, feasting, promising and lying, as with us, they take muskets and bayonets, and seizing upon the presidio and customhouse, divide the spoils and declare a new policy." Punishment for crimes varied, he said, depending on the social and political status of the perpetrators. "Of the poor Indians, very little care is taken."

This Pilgrim *replica at Dana Point gives children a taste of life at sea.*

Book-toting Dana Point statue hints of the author's snobbish trait.

He found California "blessed with a climate, than which there can be no better in the world; free from all manner of diseases . . . and with a soil in which corn yields from seventy to eighty fold," and added, "In the hands of an enterprising people, what a country this might be!"

Dana learned the hard way about the rigors of a life at sea. Before first boarding the *Pilgrim* he had relished the prospect of reading and lounging on the deck after completing his chores. He quickly discovered a seaman's duties, many of them dangerous, lasted from dawn to dusk. At night, nearly everyone took turns on watch. Sunday might be a day of leisure if the weather, the ship's whereabouts and the whims of the captain permitted.

The *Pilgrim* had first anchored at Santa Barbara on January 14, 1835, then sailed to Monterey a few days later. Her cargo ranged from casks of spirits to hardware and fireworks to jewelry. Dana and his shipmates rowed the Californians back and forth to the ship for a ten day shopping spree. The customers came mostly from the large rancheros. They searched for colorful costumes and accessories in a land where parties and wedding celebrations required finery and endurance, since they typically lasted three days.

For the return trip to Boston, the crew filled the hold with 30,000 cattle hides, toting them on their heads, one or two at a time, down to the beach, then wading out to waiting boats that often as not bobbed about. The boats carried the stiff hides to the ship, which might be anchored as much as three miles away. When a seaman slipped and the hide got wet, it was rejected. "They were very large and heavy, and nearly as stiff as boards," Dana said. "It was always wet work, and if the beach was stony, bad for our feet; for we, of course, always went barefoot."

For four months in San Diego he worked with a hide curing crew. The hides arrived sun-dried, were soaked in ocean water, brought back for another soaking in brine water, then staked out flat so meat, fat and protuding parts could be trimmed. After three strenuous weeks, "I . . . could keep up with others and clean my proportion — twenty-five," he stated.

Cattle hides and tallow were about the only exports during the Mexican period in California from 1822 to 1846.

Dana summed up the effects of Mexico's Secularization Act of 1833 as "A law stripping (the missions) of all their possessions and confining the priests to their spiritual duties; and at the same time declaring all the Indians free and independent Rancheros." Many Indians, however, remained virtual slaves, the priests lacked power and the "possessions of the missions are given over to be preyed upon by the harpies of the civil power . . . who usually end, in a few years, by making themselves fortunes."

As a result, "Trade was much diminished, credit impaired, and the venerable missions (are) going down to decay."

After returning to Boston, Dana enjoyed a hero's welcome by his Harvard schoolmates late in 1836. He earned a law degree and, between cases, became involved in politics. A California follow-up visit in 1859 revealed no changes in the tiny town of San Diego. The hide houses were gone, "But the coyotes bark still in the woods," he wrote.

Richard Henry Dana died on January 6, 1882 in Rome where he had traveled to write about international law.

Dana worked for four months in the hide houses, shown in this William Meyers water color. Dana rather liked the independence and novelty of the assignment, including working with four Kanakas, as Hawaiians were called.

Helen Hunt Jackson:
The frustrated creator of *Ramona*

"Those people are savages. You can't trust them."

People voiced reactions like these to Helen Hunt Jackson after her book about the plight of the American Indians came out in 1881. In *A Century of Dishonor* she described how the United States government had deceived the Indians by breaking promises and ignoring treaties.

Much to her dismay, a large share of the public still believed, "The only good Indian is the dead Indian." People remembered the cruelty of some Indians in their raids and warfare. Others reaped profits from lands the Indians once tilled. And since Indians could not vote, Congress ignored the book which Jackson at her own expense had sent to each member.

A Century of Dishonor was the work by which she wanted the world to judge her, but it was a romantic novel, *Ramona*, that made the New England native famous. This first novel about Southern California has gone through forty-one printings, been adapted for three movies and one stage play and is the subject of a pageant each spring in Hemet, eighty miles north of San Diego. In San Pasqual Valley, the town of Ramona (pop. 4,200) perpetuates the name.

The book's heroine, a half-breed brought up by a Mexican family, falls in love with Allessandro, an Indian. Their romance unfolds in what now seems a trite, sentimentalized idyl that

Seen by others as a woman with a cold, reserved, commanding air, Helen Hunt Jackson warmed up when it came to work. She wrote Ramona *in four months.*

darkens amid the mistreatment of Indians and the hero's death.

Jackson hoped her novel would bring the same outcry for fair treatment of Indians that *Uncle Tom's Cabin* by Harriett Beacher Stowe achieved for blacks. *Ramona* aroused sympathy and concern, but little action. "It's most enduring effect was to merely create a collection of regional myths that stimulated the tourist trade," observed Walton Bean and James Rawls in *California: An Interpretive History.* "The legends became so ingrained in the culture of Southern California that they were often mistaken for realities."

There was an irony to Jackson's role as champion of the underdog. A critic of the women's suffrage movement, indifferent to abolition, she also harbored prejudice against Catholics. In her first encounter with California Indians she thought them "hideous," said Richard Dillon in *Humbugs and Heroes.*

But changes came at a meeting in Boston in 1879. The speaker,

Chief Standing Bear, described how his Ponco tribe suffered when forced from its Dakota's Black Hills lands by agents of the United States government after gold had been discovered nearby. Promises were broken. Hardships on a mid-winter trip to the barren new reservation and the hardships there resulted in the deaths of one-hundred and fifty tribe members, including two of his own children.

Jackson immediately pitched in. She helped collect funds. She wrote articles. She persuaded friends to act. "I have become what I have said a thousand times was the most odious thing in the world, 'a woman with a hobby,' but I cannot help it."

She pestered the Department of Indian Affairs until she was appointed a special commissioner. Her assignment: to report on the conditions of the California mission Indians and find out if suitable lands were available for them. In the San Diego area, Father Anthony D. Ubach, the priest in charge of an Old Town parish, escorted her to ranches and some of the missions. He served as the model for the despairing padre in *Ramona*.

Part of the Indians' predicament in California traced back to Mexico's Secularization Act of 1833. One plan called for the Indians to acquire half the mission property with the proviso they could never sell it. Many of them, however, never learned of the plan and left to join other tribes. Some tried farming near the missions but with indifferent results. Others sank into lives of squalor and drunkenness.

The mission padres warned that the Indians were not ready to govern themselves and would be exploited after the missionairies were replaced with secular parish priests. Critics like Juan Bautista Alvarado said the missionairies themselves were to blame. They were leaving the Indians " . . . half-stupified, very much reduced in numbers, and duller than when they found them." Alvarado, it should be noted, as a native of California and one of its governors, would obtain large land grants for himself and his cronies when mission lands were parceled out.

Jackson's report on the Indians' status went back to Washington, D. C. where Congressmen ignored it. That is when the idea for *Ramona* germinated. After the book appeared in 1884, reviewers and many book buyers gave the serious message short shrift. Instead, they focused on the romance.

"It is a dead failure," said Jackson. In fact, though, more than

Loretta Young starred with Don Ameche in a 1936 20th Century Fox film based on Ramona. *It "doesn't wear well," said one critic who reviewed it in the mid-1980s.*

600,000 copies sold in the next six decades. The popularity of her poetry, travel sketches and children's books, faded, however. A short novel, *Mercy Philbrick's Choice*, interests scholars as a fictional study of poet Emily Dickinson. She was Jackson's neighbor and schoolmate in Amherst, Massachusetts.

Jackson once wrote her, "It is a cruel wrong to your day and generation that you will not give (your poems) light." She finally persuaded Dickinson to let her submit one anonymously. Jackson made two changes in the poem before mailing it.

Helen Hunt Jackson died in San Francisco at the age of fifty-five. Her last letter was sent to President Grover Cleveland with an appeal to read *A Century of Dishonor*. "I am dying happier," she added, "in the belief I have that it is your hand that is destined to strike the first steady blow toward lifting the burden of infamy from our country and righting the wrongs of the Indian race."

That appeal, like *Ramona*, had little of its intended effect.

Jesse Shepard:
The peculiar genius

O n a cool, sunny day in March 1987, the sound of a tinny Lizst concerto permeated the seedy neighborhood. Then the source of the music — an ice cream truck— rolled into view as a pair of tourists gawked at the ornate home known as Villa Montezuma in San Diego.

One could easily imagine the Villa Montezuma's original owner, Jesse Shepard, enjoying a chuckle at the effect of the moving musical interlude, for he often surprised his guests a century earlier with his musical genius and with unexpected sound effects.

Before coming to San Diego in 1887 he had visited Russia where he became intrigued by individuals who conducted seances in which communication took place, they claimed, with departed souls. He stayed a while so he could study how this was done.

San Diegans found him fascinating because of his piano playing, his singing and an unlimited degree of self-confidence. There also existed an aura of mystery about a past that included influences of spiritualism, theosophy and communication with Egyptian people no longer on an earthly plane.

During the day the local residents and speculators from other places bought and sold real estate in a dizzying spiral of frenetic hustle, then the fortunate few enjoyed the classics and improvisational mastery Shepard held over the ivories. William High recalled:

"Shepard stood in the dark with his back to the piano. Then far off voices were heard like a choir coming down the street. They came nearer and nearer until they seemed to be in the same room. They died out gradually, till only the piano was heard. Then the piano stopped, the lights came on, and there was Shepard, standing and bowing to his audience. He was a peculiar genius; I never understood how he worked it."

The sessions aroused no messages from the past nor vibrating tables, although Shepard admitted that departed pianists and composers sometimes used him as a channel of expression.

One of his hands could span an octave and a half. His courtly, genteel manner and a dreamy-eyed ascetic look entranced the city's upper crust. And the ancient Egyptians upon whom he relied for other-world conversations proved discreet. So quickly did fortunes accumulate in those days, John and William High, who were well-to-do ranchers, could shell out $19,000 for Villa Montezuma.

The architectural firm of Comstock and Trotsche borrowed from and adapted Victorian and Queen Anne styles for an ostentatious statement. The pink motif of the reception room was complemented by Persian rugs, and an art glass window featured flowers and grapes. In the music room, which takes up the east side of the house, guests relaxed and enjoyed stained glass window replicas of Beethoven, Mozart, Raphael and Rubens, plus the poet Sappho.

During the two years Shepard lived there, a polar bear skin rug dominated a section of the room. The musician slept in the red room and the gold room housed his expensively bound books on art, music and the classics. The museum and art gallery on the second floor included gifts from European monarchs. Painstakingly restored under the leadership of the San Diego Historical Society, the house is located at 1925 K Street, two blocks east of Highway I-5.

During his two-year stopover in San Diego, Shepard began writing under the name of Francis Grierson. Commentary on literature and philosophy was interspersed with critiques of materialism and the scientific approach, according to Dr. Clare Crane, in the Spring/Summer 1987 issue of *The Journal of San Diego History*. Shepard's writing style especially appealed to the intelligentsia of

Gifted pianist and singer Jesse Shepard added special effects at his concerts. The innovations stemmed from his study of seance sessions in Europe.

Villa Montezuma, built in 1887 and restored a hundred years later, boasts a lavish interior plus a Queen Anne and Victorian blend on the outside.

Europe where he had once performed for the prince of Wales and czar of Russia.

In 1888 Shepard visited France and arranged for the publication of some essays, then came back to San Diego and sold the Villa Montezuma for $29,000. He returned to Europe and continued writing until World War I persuaded him America was a superior haven. He died in 1927 at the conclusion of a piano recital benefit. He was seventy-nine. A few San Diego old-timers, upon hearing the news, could treasure memories of a two-year infusion of culture and savoir faire in what had been an artistically barren landcape.

"His legacy to San Diego, the elegant Villa Montezuma, flourishes again as a center for art and music, with exhibitions, recitals, poetry readings and receptions . . . Jesse Shepard should be very pleased," concluded Dr. Crane.

Irving J. Gill:
His simplicity created problems

His pride probably showed as architect Irving J. Gill escorted the owner of the project on a tour. Gill had used the relatively new tilt-slab construction technique that saved time and money. A pleasing blend of history and romance resulted from a design influenced by the Spanish missions in California. Each unit's small garden led into the central community garden.

The owner's reaction went like this: "Irving, by gosh, you've outdone yourself. This is supposed to house poor people, but it looks good enough to belong on the Riviera."

As one of the first West Coast architects to tackle projects for low-income people, farm laborers and company town workers, Gill achieved his goal of creating housing that added to their self respect. But on the 1910 project that so impressed the owner, Gill ended up angry. The owner jacked up the rents above the level poor people could afford because it appealed to affluent buyers.

A model company town plan at Torrance proved upsetting, too. Workers had completed ten of the concrete units, then walked off the job. Gill's simple, efficient design had eliminated a lot of traditional time-consuming tasks that labor regarded as a bread and butter issue. The work stoppage forced a return to conventional wood frame and wood paneling.

Gill encountered another frustration with the 1915 Panama-California Exposition. San Diego hired brothers John and Frederick Olmsted from Massachusetts to design the Expo and the park landscaping. The initial plan called for simple mission style buildings on the outer edges of the park, thus preserving the

*An experimenter who blended crafts-
manship and art in his projects, architect Irving Gill also used the lines of
the "expressive" missions, which retained tradition, history and romance.
He rates as one of San Diego's top
architects even though he didn't go
beyond high school in his studies.*

*Described as a romanticist, Irving Gill hit his stride with the Melville Klauber house
in 1908. Uncluttered walls and neat openings were features he would use frequently.*

incomparable views. A Boston architect, Bertram G. Goodhue, however, convinced the Expo committee to select his Spanish Mediterranean buildings in the middle of the park. Gill, who had been hired as his assistant, and the Olmsted brothers resigned. The fair's success brought Goodhue's ornate architectural style into prominence. Gill soon moved to Los Angeles.

Something he'd written helps gauge the disappointment he must have felt: "If we, the architects of the West, wish to do great works we must dare to be simple, must have the courage to fling aside every device that distracts the eye from the structural beauty, must break through conventions and get down to fundamental truths."

Gill learned basic skills working with his hands on his father's farm near Tully, New York, where he was born in 1870. After his older brother John became a building contractor, Gill could see more clearly that farming could never be his life's work. With high school diploma in hand he headed toward Chicago for the architectural firm of Adler & Sullivan after a short stopover in Syracuse.

Fortunately for him, old man Sullivan viewed college as a waste of time. He hired the young man and discovered he knew something about how a building is built, didn't rely on frills and had an eye for the compatability of buildings to their surroundings. Gill learned that he was free to ignore the prevailing Roman form and turn instead at times to African architecture, adapting the country's uncluttered walls, earth contours and colorful decorations.

Gill chose San Diego as an ideal place when his health forced a move in 1893, a year when the entire country's economic health suffered. He joined in a partnership, branched out on his own, then in 1897 teamed with William S. Hebbard who favored sturdy, shingled English structures. Within a few years, Gill's work reflected the harmonious blend of the adobe missions to their horizontal settings. In 1907 he joined forces for a year with Frank Mead, a man interested in ancient architecture.

Gill came into his own with the design for the Melville Klauber house, completed in San Diego in 1908. Its smooth surfaces and uncluttered Spanish arches and openings became his graceful trademarks. The unpretentious approach maintained tradition but with originality.

Contractors even in those days were hard to pin down, so Gill set up his own concrete construction firm intended for the tilt-slab walls and other concrete sections he favored. The venture, however, almost bankrupted him. For color, shade and fragrance, Gill paid special attention to his garden planning. He hired Kate Sessions, the landscape gardener busy transforming Balboa Park, for some of his best projects and piqued interest with garden tiles shaped in Arabic patterns. He also lavished attention on his interiors.

Many of Gill's buildings and homes still enhance the San Diego area scene: the original Scripps Institute of Oceanography building and the Ellen B. Scripps' home in La Jolla; in San Diego the Christian Science Church at Second and Laurel.

He returned to San Diego from Los Angeles in 1920 and continued designing buildings and homes until shortly before his death in 1936. His passion for simplicity requires a discerning eye, because the buildings he designed usually blend so well with their surroundings.

A jewel for Horton Plaza visitors, this Irving Gill fountain was donated to the city by Louis J. Wilde, who kept both supporters and opponents guessing by his unpredictable behavior when he served as San Diego's mayor.

Madam Ernestine Schumann-Heink:
Opera's ugly duckling

A **critic** once described her as "The ugliest woman to ever tread a stage." In her teens an opera director told her after an audition, "Go home, quick, and ask your kind friends who helped you come to Vienna to buy you instead a sewing machine." In America, physically beyond the "stout" size, she became stuck one night in a narrow backstage doorway. "Try turning sideways, madam," a stagehand said. "Young man," she gasped, "can't you see I haff no sidevays."

What she did "haff" just happened to be the greatest contralto voice of her generation, with a range from low D to high C, a natural talent for acting and a personality that charmed both individuals and crowds. At the 1915 Panama-California Exposition in San Diego, 28,000 people jammed Balboa Park to hear her. During World War I, she performed before countless groups of servicemen. She brought tears to their eyes with "Silent Night." They called her "mother" and later voted her an honorary Amercian Legion officer.

If the war hadn't interrupted, she might have made San Diego an

God loves who can laugh!
So laugh dear herr fletcher.
your old
Schumann Heink

As a young mother in Germany, Ernestine Heink contemplated suicide. Her grit and buoyancy, evidenced in this note to Ed Fletcher, helped her through the crisis.

American Bayreuth with an annual week-long festival of opera and the classics, much like the musical performances each summer in the German town where composer Richard Wagner lived. The plan evolved after she made San Diego home in 1912. Real estate developer William B. Gross made her location decision easier: he gave her several acres atop present day Grossmont in exchange for her help in establishing an artists colony. It got off to a fast start, but two of the luminaries died in their prime and America's entry in the war on April 6, 1917 torpedoed the musical gala she'd planned for that year and in 1918.

The war caused personal anguish. One of her sons felt compelled to fight for his fatherland's cause and died as a German soldier.

Another son died as an American doughboy. The loss of her sons, the death of her second husband, Paul Schumann, in 1905, derision about her looks, earlier years of hardship—any one of these setbacks would have thwarted a less resilient person. Somehow she struggled through, helped by the power of Wagner's music she so dramatically performed.

"Tini" **Roessler** was born in 1861 in Austria. Her father, an Austrian army officer, scoffed at her interest in singing. Her mother, however, taught her Italian opera arias even though it seemed to Tini there was "always another baby coming." The father's miniscule army pay and the family's increasing size meant Tini often went hungry.

Through friends of her parents she obtained music lessons and at the age of fifteen signed a contract with the Dresden Royal Opera Company. She felt no fear ("Because I am homely") about being on her own in Dresden. She stayed with the widow of a cathedral organist. In her first role she played *Azvcena* in "Il Trovatore" and continued performing bit parts in later productions.

At the age of eighteen, without permission, she married Ernest Heink, the opera company's secretary. Both of them lost their jobs for their impetuosity. Despite the rapid arrival of her first three children, she landed occasional small parts, including a performance only hours before her son Hans arrived. Ernest Heink had obtained a low-paying customs house job and transferred to another city. He decided to abandon the responsibilities of parenthoood.

Broke, hungry, her three small children nearly frozen, Ernestine Heink could see no future for herself or them. With Hans in her arms and leading the two girls, she headed for the railroad track, intending to let an oncoming train end their misery. Lotta, sensing her mother's agony if not her intent, cried, "Mamma, mamma. I love you." The child's voice brought her back to her senses and for the rest of her days ruled out suicide as a way of solving problems.

Finally, her chance for stardom arrived. A contralto scheduled for the lead in "Carmen" fought with director and refused to perform in Hamburg. He called on Tini and she thrilled the audience. Once again the same sulky prima donna balked and Tini substituted in "Le Phophete," which includes one of the toughest

contralto roles in opera. Tini won an ovation. On her third pinch
hitting assignment she earned a permanent promotion. She soon
became Germany's preeminent performer.

An 1898 American tour so impressed opera goers she canceled
a lucrative Berlin contract to continue singing in the states. A
forty-thousand mile regimen that began in 1903, however, almost
ended her career. Exhausted, fearing she'd ruined her voice, she
recuperated for a year in Germany, then came back and cemented
a reputation as the world's greatest. She became a United States
citizen in 1905.

A marriage in 1906 to Chicago attorney William Rapp, Jr. lasted
only a few years. Madam Ernestine Schumann-Heink continued
performing until the age of seventy-one, shifting from heavy duty
arias to folk songs for vaudeville, radio and even one movie. She
died November 17, 1936.

Although she appeared an ugly duckling in the eyes of some
critics her beautiful voice brought joy to people from all walks of life
in America and other parts of the world.

John J. Montgomery:
An aviator who escaped oblivion

A t the first light of dawn John J. Montgomery and his brother James picked up their rifles and a thirty-eight pound bundle of wood and fabric which they hid under a layer of hay on the wagon. John had coined a word for the bundle: "aeroplane." They stashed it out of sight and toted the rifles just in case any curious neighbors inquired about their outing. In the past, some jokes and ridicule about John's experiments had made the twenty-five-year-old inventor almost reclusive. If stopped, they could say they were going rabbit hunting.

Out on the mesa's edge on the family's Otay Valley ranch, John assembled his craft. The wings were shaped like a gull's wings, as wide as a baseball coach's third base box. The brothers waited until the breezes picked up. James had tied a rope on the front and waited a dozen feet or so down the slope until John shouted, "Now!" James pulled the rope and together they ran a few steps until the "Gull Glider" was aloft. At a height of about fifteen feet, the wiry, one-hundred and thirty pound John Joseph Montgomery flew six-hundred feet to a graceful landing on an August day in 1883. It was the world's first controlled heavier-than-air flight and preceded Orville Wright's engine-driven flight by twenty years.

At a conference some years later, he described how a "bird man" felt: "I took this apparatus to the top of a hill facing a gentle wind. There was a little run and a jump and I found myself launched in the air. A peculiar sensation came over me. The first feeling in placing myself at the mercy of the wind was that of fear. Imme-

John J. Montgomery, credited with establishing the first basic principles of aero-dynamics, successfully made the first controlled heavier-than-air flight in 1883.

The scene looked much like this on Montgomery's initial glide off Otay Mesa. His ranching neighbors thought the rather reclusive fellow a bit loony.

diately after came a feeling of security when I realized the solid support given by the wing-surface. And that support was of a very peculiar nature. There was as cushiony softness about it, yet it was firm. When I found the machine would follow any movement in the seat for balancing, I felt I was self-buoyant . . . ."

The exploit and follow-up flights caused comments in the area southwest of San Diego. Later experiments up north near Santa Clara and San Jose were publicized, but Montgomery for years was virtually an unknown aviation pioneer. Even today many aviation history books neglect him. A movie, "Gallant Journey," produced by Columbia Pictures in 1946, told his story. A biography, *John J. Montgomery: Father of Basic Flying,* by Arthur D. Spearman, also helped somewhat in correcting the oversight after its publication in 1967.

Born in in Yuba City in 1858, John was five years old when the family moved to Oakland. As a toddler he liked to lie on a pillow and "pretend to fly," his mother said. He studied clouds, wondering if he could fly by catching one. He flew kites. He watched birds. At the age of eleven John joined a Fourth of July crowd in an Emeryville park as Frank Merriott piloted a steam-propelled hydrogen balloon, then the boy returned home and promptly built a model of the semi-dirigible craft.

As a young man he ferried across San Francisco Bay to attend Santa Clara University when it was still a college. He transferred to St. Ignatius in San Francisco where he obtained a Masters of Science degree. In 1883 he joined the family on a farm called Fruitland on the old Rancho Tia Juana once owned by Sandieguito Arguello.

John's father, Zachary Montgomery, had distinguished himself as a lawyer, journalist and politician, then slowed the pace down by taking up farming and publishing a weekly newspaper. Young Montgomery became foreman of the farm and promptly set up a workshop complete with a lathe in the barn. His sister Jane pumped the bellows on a steam boiler. The heat helped shape the ash strips into parabolic cambered wing ribs resembling wings of birds he had captured or shot down for his studies. The neighbors thought him a bit daft.

Montgomery continued studying and testing his aeroplanes in between college teaching assignments in Northern California. A circus daredevil who parachuted from balloons, one Dan Malone, approached him, saying, "I will have a balloon hoist me in your aeroplane to the four-thousand foot level, then I'll cut it loose and glide to the ground." Malone's first flight, a twenty minute graceful descent, was a delight to behold. The second time in 1905 a dangling balloon release cable tangled above Malone's head out of sight. He died in the crash, with a gallant wave just before the impact.

After recovering from the tragedy, Montgomery resumed his flights. A doctor advised him when he was fifty-three that he should stay on the ground. Montgomery wanted one more time for an evaluation of some changes he had made in his latest craft. It stalled, side slipped and crashed. He died before a doctor could reach the scene.

His findings and airplane designs finally earned him a well-deserved place with Octave Chanute and Dr. Samuel Pierpont Langley as American pioneers in controlled flight before the Wright brothers accomplished their Kitty Hawk milestone.

Glenn H. Curtiss:
A modest aviation pioneer

On the city's side of San Diego Bay, it probably sounded like three mosquitoes attacking the Coronado polo grounds. Actually, the buzzing came from the sixty-horsepower, eight-cylinder engines in three flying machines. They belonged to Glenn H. Curtiss, ex-bicycle shop proprietor and a champion racer of bicycles, motorcycles and aeroplanes.

His two-day flying exhibit over Coronado in 1911 helped establish the modest, thirty-two-year-old New Yorker not only as an expert pilot and manufacturer of flying machines but a top notch instructor as well.

The planes approached sixty miles per hour in the races. A crowd of nearly 10,000 people oohed and aahed on Sunday, January 29, as the planes almost grazed the water and climbed until specks against an overcast sky. The skills of the three military "bird men" proved the Curtiss Aviation School's competence.

Three days earlier, Curtiss had taxied his hydro-aeroplane into the Spanish Bight, a protected section of water between the tip of Point Loma and the coastline. With the engine wide open he skimmed along at forty miles an hour, lifted off the water once, twice, then roared aloft on the world's first water-to-air flight.

A month later he again zoomed aloft, then landed the plane in San Diego Bay and taxied next to the cruiser *Pennsylvania*. Its giant crane hoisted the biplane aboard as it were a toy, then lowered it back over the side. This was the only maneuver, the Secretary of Navy had said, that would convince him aeroplanes offered practical benefits for the fleet. In May he authorized the purchase of the Navy's first two planes—from Curtiss.

Another daring feat brought Curtiss Exhibition Company employee Eugene B. Ely into prominence. "Give me enough power and I will fly a barn door," he once said. Carpenters had built a platform one-hundred and twenty-five feet long—the distance from a home plate to second base—above deck on the man of war *Pennsylvania*. On Janury 18, 1911 Ely landed his pusher-style flying machine on the ship while she was anchored in San Francisco Bay.

A year earlier Ely flew off a similar platform on the *Birmingham*, sagged almost to water level, then regained height and landed two miles away near Norfolk, Virginia. It was another aviation first in a Curtiss-built craft that today would be called a motorized kite.

After the two-day Coronado flying exhibit, the San Diego Aero Club helped persuade John D. Spreckels to give Curtiss free use of North Island for three years. Curtiss told Army and Navy officials he would train recruits free the first year and thus ushered in the nation's first military aviation school. Theodore G. Ellyson, fresh from three years in the submarine boat service, became the Navy's first pilot.

In three years the school's instructors trained fliers from India, Japan and Greece along with Americans willing to pay six-hundred dollars for hydro-aeroplane or five-hundred dollars for conventional craft training. Students, alumni and staff achieved some notable "firsts"—the first aerial photos, a loop-the-loop, an aerial bombing run, night flying and an altitude record of 16,800 feet. After the third year, the Army Signal Corps took over and named the site Rockwell Field.

One of those rare individuals able to repair, build and operate almost any type of machine, Glenn Hammond Curtiss was born in Hammondsport, New York, in 1878. His father died when the boy was four. Glenn's humility often prompted a desire in others to lend him a hand.

In the bike shop he opened, his former boss complained about the exertion of peddling a bike uphill. Curtiss, then twenty-two, originated a small booster motor, which quickly turned into a profitable sideline business. Meanwhile he switched from racing bicycles to racing motorcycles, setting speed records on nearly

At full throttle, this Curtiss Exhibition Co. Bird Man reached almost 60 miles per hour above North Island in a 1911 air show—the area's first.

Glenn Curtiss, at the controls of one of his earliest hydro-aeroplanes, eventually convinced the Navy amphibious craft could play a vital military role.

every course he navigated. His skill in building lightweight motors for balloonists landed him a contract for Army dirigible motors. These aroused Alexander Graham Bell's interest. The inventor of the telephone joined with Curtiss and several other men in an Aerial Experiment Association in October 1907. They began building planes, adapting ideas of the Wright brothers and Gabriel Voisin, a French innovator. Curtiss conceived the *June Bug*, a biplane in which he won the first leg of a *Scientific American* cup race. In August, 1909, he captured a Reims, France, air meet prize for achieving forty-three miles per hour. The following year he won again in Los Angeles with a record-setting fifty-five miles an hour.

The plane that clinched his manufacturing prowess, the JN 4D—best known as the Jenny—served as the trainer for military pilots before and during World War I, but British and French fighters proved superior in the dog fights with Germany's superb Fokker.

After the war, Curtiss retired in Florida where he dabbled in farming and concentrated on hunting birds. He lacked the financial and engineering savvy for big business wheeling and dealing. He possessed what some people lack, however—an awareness of his own limitations.

Claude Ryan:
The man with a bittersweet Lindbergh link

The future looked overcast and dreary for T. Claude Ryan at the start of 1927. He and his partner, the glad-handing B. Franklin Mahoney, had launched the nation's first year-round regularly scheduled daily airline passenger service two years earlier on March 1. The San Diego-Los Angeles flights sold out at the beginning. Then, with the novelty gone, business dropped and bankruptcy loomed. So Mahoney bought out his partner's share of Ryan Airlines, Inc.

Ryan stayed on as manager. His preoccupation with financial problems left little time for overseeing production of the Ryan M-1, the first plane of his own design. Airmail flyers liked the trim little monoplane for its rugged dependability. Despite its appeal, the trickle of M-1 orders had all but dried up.

Early in 1927 a wire arrived from Robertson Aircraft in St. Louis: "Can you construct Whirlwind engine plane capable flying nonstop between New York and Paris? Stop. If so please state cost and delivery date." The wire came from Charles A. Lindbergh, former balloonist, wing walker and airmail pilot. He put up $2,000 of his own, obtained backing from St. Louis businessmen and convinced them a single-engine plane stood the best chance for the crossing. Other fliers vying for a $25,000 prize for the first non-stop Atlantic flight had opted for multi-engine planes, some of which could not rise off the ground when their oversized tanks were filled with gasoline.

Lindbergh visited Ryan Aviation's San Diego plant, which still exuded pungent reminders of its previous use as a cannery. He felt in his bones time was running out. His first choice, the Columbia aircraft, was unobtainable, so with his options nearly nil he signed papers with the Ryan company and practically moved in. Engineer Donald A. Hall designed just what Lindbergh wanted—a flying gasoline tank almost twenty-eight feet long and with a forty-six foot wing span.

One day a careless worker dropped a crescent wrench that broke off a thumbnail-size piece of the engine's number one cooling fin. Mechanic O. L. Gray said, "We could smooth that out with a file and paint it, and never know the difference." Lindbergh said, " I'll always know the difference." After a pause he added, "We want another engine in there."

Gray thought he was kidding. Someone asked, "Why so much perfection in this?" Lindbergh had his reasons: "One is I'm a poor swimmer." In this way the work crew learned of his plans and redoubled efforts in the race against time.

Enmeshed in the firm's economic plight, Ryan rarely became involved in the craft Lindbergh called "The Spirit of St. Louis." The two men shared much in common. Both grew up in small towns: Ryan in Parsons, Kansas, and Lindbergh in Little Falls, Minnesota. They developed affinities for motorcycles, cars and finally airplanes. In San Diego Ryan bought his first aircraft, a Jenny trainer, in 1922 for four-hundred dollars. Lindbergh followed suit a year later, paying five-hundred for his Jenny. Both took flying lessons on their own, then benefited from military training schools. And both of them did stints at barnstorming, acquiring along the way know-how in matters such as forced landings, which in the early days of flying rated as routine.

Lindbergh's solo nonstop flight that began outside New York City May 20, 1927 ended thirty-three and a half hours later in Paris. Overnight he became a hero around the world. The flight also made Ryan Aviation famous. Orders for the M-1 came from all parts of the globe to a woefully unprepared company. Ryan, no longer an owner and far removed from the design or construction of "The Spirit of St. Louis," built a protective shell that shielded him from the onrush of news media inquiries about his role in the saga. He kept the shell up for years.

In 1928 Ryan formed The Ryan Aeronautical Company. His

In a life that paralleled Charles Lindbergh's, Ryan pioneered airplane designs in San Diego, but found himself outside "The Spirit of St. Louis" winner's circle.

knack for anticipating the needs and desires of fliers helped the San Diego firm survive the lean depression years. The Ryan S-T (for Sports Trainer) became the Model T of flying, except it looked much sportier. Adapted slightly, the S-T served as the preeminent trainer through World War II. In the years the followed, Ryan built

the first jet-plus-propeller aircraft for the Navy and the first success-
ful vertical takeoff and landing aircraft—the Ryan X-13 Vertijet.
His company pioneered remotely piloted vehicles and jet drones,
Doppler systems and lunar landing radar.

Like Lindbergh, Ryan ended up a wealthy and widely acclaimed
man. Teledyne, Inc. acquired Ryan's company in 1969 for $128
million.

He started out mowing lawns and delivering *The Saturday
Evening Post* for spending money. During school vacations he
drove a wagon for his father's Excelsoir Steam Laundry in Parsons,
where he was born January 3, 1898. His first regular job, a paper
route, still left time to watch repairs being made on the town's first
automobiles. Later, after the family moved to Orange, California,
he invested his savings in a motorcycle, a seven-horsepower model.

After buying his Jenny in San Diego, he charged from two-and-
a-half to five dollars a ride, using an improvised air field on the
waterfront near the foot of Broadway. Next he shifted operations to
Dutch Flats, which later would become the main Postal Service
office site. Dutch Flats served as the terminal for the airline passenger service he and Mahoney operated.

"Claude Ryan's name will probably be longer remembered for
associations with Lindbergh's plane than for many more significant
contributions he made in the half century that followed," according
to William Wagner, author of *Ryan, the Aviator*. T. Claude Ryan died
in 1982 at the age of eighty-four while he sketched a rough design
concept for a plane with simplified controls. It was a goal that
characterized his career— making flying easier for more people to
enjoy.

Reuben Fleet:
Defense contractor
with a conscience

In the fall of 1939, soon after England declared war against Germany, Reuben Fleet met his friend Admiral John Towers. The result: Fleet's winning bid for a $20 million order for five-hundred PBY-5s, the long-range patrol aircraft that later became known as the Catalina.

As the largest single contract for military planes up to that time, the deal required an advance tax agreement. Fleet flew to Washington, D. C. for a session with Admiral W. A. Moffett, General Henry "Hap" Arnold, the Internal Revenue Service commissioner and their staff members. One man began reading the agreement. After about half a dozen pages, Fleet sounded off: "How in the name of goodness do you expect me to understand what that says?" He offered the services of his own attorney who could, Fleet declared, cut the gibberish to one page.

Not possible, said the IRS chief. The man reading it, Herman Reiling, was the only person who could write the tax code.

"No wonder it is such a conglomeration," said Fleet, "if you will excuse me for saying so. If we threw the whole damn tax act in the wastebasket and started over again it would be a great deal better. Tell me, Mr. Reiling, what does it mean?"

"You're a tough hombre, Major Fleet. It means that the minute you say the job is done, you get your money."

That's all Fleet needed. He signed without listening to another word.

This anecdote comes from William Wagner's book *Reuben Fleet and the Story of Consolidated Aircraft.* It describes the major's role in helping establish the airline now known as Pan American, his airplane innovations and flying exploits.

As head of Consolidated Aircraft of San Diego, Fleet tangled with the government about its red tape, the definition of excess profits and the government's intrusion in employee relations. The government's controls on employee matters, in fact, would decide Fleet on selling his interest in Consolidated in 1941.

Fleet also battled on behalf of San Diego. A pre-World War II armament build-up created housing, water and sewage disposal needs. When a group of visiting Congressmen came to town, Fleet sheparded them onto *New Moon*, his recently acquired yacht, for an afternoon cruise on the bay. His motive surfaced when he invited guests to lean over the rail. "Now sniff!" he commanded. "Smell it? It's sewage. Evil, disease-breeding sewage, dumped in this beautiful bay because the City of San Diego has no funds for a proper disposal plant."

A few days later he learned government funds would be forthcoming for a new sewage plant.

To say Fleet was outspoken is putting it mildly. Sir Arthur Harris, England's Royal Air Force marshall, presumably had him in mind when describing the American plane manufacturer "afflicted with verbal diarhea." Admiral Towers, faced with a hectic schedule, once removed the chairs from his office before Fleet arrived. But Fleet, ignoring the hint, perched on a corner of the admiral's desk and chattered for two hours. If introduced or asked to say a few words to a group, Fleet usually embarked on a non-stop course, or so it seemed to his audiences. "Can't someone shut him off?" was a typical plaint.

With all that talk, though, came action. As a defense contractor he ordered the words "Nothing short of right is right" painted in

Reuben H. Fleet as he appeared during World War I service as a major.

nine-foot-high letters under a plant roof line. He insisted on living up to the saying even when it required more dollars than expected. "The way to stay in business with the Army and Navy," Fleet said, "is to give them your best without any holding back."

In the early days at Consolidated he gambled that the "Husky" trainer would win repeat orders, so he bought extra supplies. Sure enough, more orders arrived. One result: The Army charged him with making excess profits and required fifty more planes—free. Fleet fumed. Finally he settled on a price: one dollar per plane. He complained that the government set a ten percent ceiling on profit, but never made up the difference when a manufacturer made less than that.

When his company moved from Buffalo to San Diego in 1935, he set up a continuous flowline from raw materials to assembled product. He nurtured David R. Davis' idea for a wing airfoil, which improved aircraft performance twenty percent. Fleet initiated the first use of rockets for heavily laden planes on takeoffs. Consolidated's output of of B-24 bombers topped the entire industry in World War II, according to Wagner's biography.

Fleet exhibited business savvy at the age of ten in Montesano, Washington, where he was born in 1887. He persuaded his mother to send away for a setting of Peacomb Plymouth Rocks— the Cadillacs of the poultry field. He soon developed a booming business throughout Chehalis County. His interest in flying evolved early, too. He once rigged a set of wings from old sheets, dove off the barn and fell more like a rock than a bird into the hay stack he had wisely targeted for a landing.

His parents expected him to excel. At Culver Military Academy where his uncle Fred superintended, he became "Reub" and captained the debate team, edited the newspaper, starred in football, track and baseball. He graduated second in his class. (Uncle Fred feared talk of nepotism if his nephew ranked first, even though he had earned it.)

The young man returned home and taught school. Next he worked for his father who operated an abstract company. This led to Fleet's own successful real estate business. National Guard duty helped him learn to fly and World War I brought him into prominence, first in flight training, then as the officer in charge of the

PT-3 "Husky" produced by Reuben Fleet's Consolidated Aircraft plant became the standard trainer for Army and Navy pilots between World Wars I and II.

nation's first air mail service, which the Army briefly operated.

At times considerate, even sentimental, Fleet also could cow a supplier or an employee with his temper. He once swept everything off his desk, including the ink, when his secretary declared she could not work overtime. "He wasn't ashamed of his outbursts; he rather gloried in being able to get away with them," said a woman who worked on the McCook Field staff in Dayton, Ohio, during his 1919-22 stint in charge of the Army Air Service's engineering division.

Fleet died October 29, 1975 at the age of eighty-eight, just twenty-four days before he was to be inducted into the Aviation Hall of Fame. The Reuben H. Fleet Space Theater & Science Center in Balboa Park keeps his memory alive. It was the first theater/planetarium to be built in the United States.

An engineer in the U.S. Topographical Corps — the cream of the Army's departments — Lt. George Derby freelanced as a writer of humorous sketches and kept friends in a state of uneasy wariness with his penchant for practical jokes.

Lt. George Horatio Derby:
Prankster of renown

Hardship, avarice and isolation. These were among the companions of many early American settlers after they reached California. These grim sidekicks help explain why newcomers placed a premium on humor. And the appreciation of it explains why so many of them began to enjoy the wit and, when they were played on others, the practical jokes of Lieutenant George Horatio Derby.

He was one of California's first humorists. And as with nearly all luminaries, fictitious stories sprouted about him. One dealt with the reason for his transfer West. Headquarters assigned him, so the tale goes, to survey the Tombigbee River "to see how far up it runs." Lt. Derby supposedly responded in great detail how he had studied the river and its adjoining topography. He even interviewed settlers along the river's banks in Alabama and Mississippi.

"My conclusion," he wrote, "is that the Tombigbee River does not run up, but down."

Secretary of War Jefferson Davis reportedly was not amused. Soon the lieutenant was sweating with General Bennett Riley and his men exploring the Sacramento and San Joaquin valleys. Then on to even hotter terrain — Fort Yuma in California's Imperial County, just across the border from Yuma, Arizona. His "exile" there didn't diminish his penchant for practical jokes and witticisms.

"One of our Fort Yuma men died," Derby would tell newcomers, "and unfortunately went to hell. He wasn't there one day before he telegraphed for his blankets."

Cooler climes didn't change him. At a rousing ball in Sonoma, Derby's brainstorm was to switch two babies and their toys and blankets into each other's basket, so their parents took home the wrong infants after the party ended. Owen Wister borrowed the incident for use in his novel *The Virginian*, according to the entertaining *John Phoenix, Esq.*, which George R. Stewart chose as the title of Derby's biography.

Derby transferred to San Diego shortly before he turned thirty. Word soon circulated that he was building a dike alongside the San Diego River instead of across it, perhaps as revenge for his transfer. This project wasn't a joke, though. A crackerjack engineer in the United States Army Corps of Topographical Engineers, Derby was following orders to shift the river back to its original bed and thus solve the silt build-up in the harbor.

He supplemented his Army pay with surveying jobs so that he and Mary Coons could marry in 1854. The record fails to show what pranks were played on the newlyweds, but like so many practical jokers, Derby failed to see the humor in it when the joke was on him.

One idea occurred to him before riding in a carriage with two other passengers. He confided to each of them in turn, "Oh, by the way, our other passenger is almost stone deaf." Then he sat back poker-faced during the shouting match that followed.

With a young man named James Sherman as his accomplice, Derby set up Don Julio Carillo of Sonora, a man who heard the pair extolling the Masons. "I would like to join," said Carillo. "Fine," Derby said, "but you realize all new members must be branded with a new steel branding iron?" Carillo considered this a moment, then agreed, saying, "Esta bueno."

Sherman rounded up the branding iron plus a piece of cowhide with hair on it. He blindfolded the don, but not until the initiate had seen the iron turn red in the forge. Derby threw the cowhide into the flames for a suitable aroma and pressed the branding iron onto Carillo. He had, however, first inserted a piece of wet paper between the skin and the iron. So the victim felt the heat but escaped a burn. "Es bastante," Carillo bravely cried. When he saw his unblemished skin he was prepared to announce a miracle.

The lieutenant defused one near-calamity. Two associates decided a duel would settle their argument, so Derby molded their bullets out of tallow and added charcoal for color. Instead of killing or maiming each other, the opponents simply splattered themselves.

Derby was born in Massachusetts in 1823. His deviltry surfaced in an austere, pious but loving home atmosphere. During three years in a boy's academy, a harsh superintendent tried unsuccessfully to beat the bent for jokes out of him.

Writing proved another source of income for the lowly paid lieutenant. His newspaper columns ended up in book form and both *Phoenixiana* and *The Squibob Papers* enjoyed good sales until their characters and topical references became outdated. His writing skill served Derby well in August 1853 when John Judson Ames, editor of the weekly four-page *San Diego Herald*, asked him to keep an eye on things at the paper while he went to a Democratic Party meeting in San Francisco.

Soon editorial page readers who had been urged to elect the Democratic candidate for governor found themselves being asked to switch their support to the Whig candidate, one William Waldo, who later ended up carrying San Diego, much to Ames' discomfiture.

Derby predicted in print what the future held for him when the six-foot, six-inch Ames returned: "We held (Ames) down over the press by our nose (which we had inserted between his teeth for that purpose) and while our hair was employed in holding one of his hands, we held the other in our left and . . . shouted to him, 'Say Waldo!' "

Derby surveyed military roads in Oregon and Washington Territory. He wrote, "It rains incessantly twenty-six hours a day for seventeen months of the year."

Next he headed for New York in 1856 where, despite illness and partial blindness, he managed to play a few more pranks. After his death in 1861 at the age of thirty-eight, a friend had this to say: "What other men would sacrifice for ambition, for love, for the attainment of fortune or personal aggrandizement, he would sacrifice for fun — his best friend would have no more chance of escape than his worst enemy."

Shrewd and competitive, Edward Scripps used eccentric behavior as a ploy; it brought a laugh or pity instead of the enmity that many people in power encounter.

The generous eccentrics

W hen his father took to bed with a debilitating illness, four-teen-year-old Eddie Scripps inherited the job of field fore-man at the family's Rushville, Illinois, farm. Hired hands in 1870 earned one dollar a day. That amount threatened the family savings as planting time neared.

Eddie hit upon an idea. He obtained permission from his father to round up some town boys instead of hiring men. The slender red-haired lad hired a crew, spaced off rows in the field, then started the lads in a series of hoeing races. Eddie shouted encouragement, fanning their competitive spirit.

"Soon enough I had my book out . . . and was in a fence corner reading," he recalled in his memoirs, *Damned Old Crank*. "I told the boys to call me when they got on their last rows so that I could overlook their work." He paid them twenty-five cents a day.

Edward Wyllis Scripps exhibited shrewdness like this on both the business and editorial sides of the forty newspapers he ended up owning. The chain provided a fortune that enabled Scripps and his half-sister Ellen Browning Scripps to found and support San Diego area institutions which continue supplying benefits today. And his sister Virginia left her own indelible impression on La Jolla.

Scripps left the farm at the age of eighteen and worked on the Detroit newspaper owned and operated by his brother James. The rookie developed a knack for selling subscriptions and soon hired ten youngsters to deliver papers to the customers he had landed. He made three or four times the money reporters earned. Nonethe-less, he coveted their roles. By taking on their most disagreeable reporting chores, he won a beat of his own, then moved up to city editor.

When he reached the age of twenty-four, with backing from

Quiet, often reclusive, Ellen Scripps became an early woman columnist, earned a fortune from investments in the Scripps publishing empire and gave much of it away.

James and other relatives, he established the *Cleveland Penny Press*. He underpriced the competition and, in a time when reporters loaded down their readers with verbose writing, attracted subscribers with condensed stories. As he began buying out or starting new papers, he granted forty-nine percent of the ownership to staff members and retained the rest. Easy-to-read articles and the efforts of gung-ho staffs usually hiked circulation. Increased advertising revenue followed.

Scripps had more than earned his first million by the age of thirty-six when he relocated. He chose an arid mesa sixteen miles north of San Diego and paid $5,000 for four-hundred acres, which he called Miramar Ranch. He wielded control over his newspaper chain by memos, letters and issued edicts in person to a steady stream of visiting aides and editors.

Ellen Browning Scripps lent him part of the $5,000 for the ranch. She also helped bankroll a brother, Fred, for an unsuccessful lemon and orange tree grove. E. W. Scripps threw himself into landscaping and road building projects, adding another 1,700 acres in the process. One road led to San Diego, which he described as "a busted broken down boom town" in 1890.

Ellen Scripps exerted an unusual influence over Eddie when he was "a sickly, whining and unhappy child," as he recalled. She had graduated from college, the only child of the family who did so, when he was four, and began reading aloud to him. Four years later she introduced him to Shakespeare.

She also worked for the newspaper, beginning as a proofreader, then becoming one of the country's first woman columnists. Over the years she invested wisely. As the dividends flowed in, she started giving money away. A few of the beneficiaries included the La Jolla Women's Club and the city's library, the Episcopalian Bishop's School for girls, the Scripps Memorial Hospital and Metabolic Clinic. She and E. W. donated most of the money for the establishment of the Scripps Institution of Oceanography.

Virginia Scripps probably influenced them on supporting the institution. She loved the sea, the desert, the town of La Jolla and the color purple. Miss Virginia, as everyone called her, minced no words about people who displeased her. A former neighbor, Mrs. Bartlette, once said:

"In the middle of church one morning a car started backfiring loudly outside. It kept clanging and chugging, so Miss Virginia marched out, stood by the church door and motioned the driver over. He drove across the street with the car still backfiring and she shouted, 'What the hell do you think you're doing? Don't you know we're trying to pray in here?'"

Judith Morgan included this quote in her July 30, 1967 *San Diego Union* article called "The Miss Scripps Nobody Knows."

Miss Virginia often served as a self-appointed church usher. When people became ill she took them home and nursed them back to recovery, and if she heard about a family in need she sent a basket of food. She donated the land on which St. James-By-the-Sea Episcopal Church was built.

At the train station one day, Miss Virginia arrived to see a friend off, but one suitcase had been forgotten. Miss Virginia promptly hired a lad to retrieve the bag, grabbed a suitcase and parked herself on top of it in front of the locomotive. There she remained until her friend boarded the train — with all her luggage.

A typical day began with Miss Virginia making the rounds downtown wearing a pith helmet and putting litter into her wheelbarrow. Pity the poor wretch who littered in her vicinity: she would run after the culprit, brandishing a stick.

The mother of Edward and Miss Virginia was of Irish and Scotch origin and Ellen's mother was English. According to Judith Morgan's feature, Miss Virginia explained her brazenness by saying, "Ellen's mother was a lady and mine wasn't."

Her half-sister, Ellen Scripps, frugal about personal spending, gave away most of her fortune. Ellen was four when her mother died and her grandmother cared for her. At a boarding school, a strict, sanctimonious teacher humiliated her. This caused such a dread of ridicule she avoided situations that held any risk of a repeat occurence. She died at the age of ninety in 1932.

E. W. Scripps prided himself on revitalizing the United Press Association at a time when the Associated Press seemed intent on a monopoly service for morning papers. He established the Science News Service, which made technical information understandable

Outspoken and uninhibited, Virginia Scripps believed men were good for one thing — to swear at. She was a one-woman anti-litter bug.

to laymen. His papers fought for the rights of common people and for labor.

Acquire a reputation for eccentricity, he recommended. That way, your striving for success will excite "mirth and perhaps pity," instead of enmity. It's a formula that worked at least part of the time for him and his sister Miss Virginia.

Mixing his special rainmaking chemicals for a magazine photographer, Charles Hatfield, a staunch Quaker, revealed his neatness of dress. He matched it with integrity in dealing with others, said reporter Thomas W. Patterson.

Charles M. Hatfield:
The moisturizer man

Real estate agent Fred A. Binney, a member in good standing of the San Diego Wide Awake Improvement Club, sent a letter to the city council. With support from some of his club members, he offered the following suggestions:

The Morena Dam reservoir is barely one-third full and the city's growth hinges on an ample water supply. We think the council should consider hiring Charles M. Hatfield to make some rain fall.

This was in 1912. The council members thanked Binney and his club for the idea. Yes, it was dry and, yes, they had heard about Mr. Hatfield, but since his rainmaking techniques could not be proved scientifically, the council could not authorize taxpayers' money for such a scheme.

Lots of people in Southern California knew about Hatfield, who by then rated folk hero status. He called himself the Moisture Accelerator, but others knew him best as The Rainmaker. Since 1902 when his first experiments with chemicals and "evaporating tanks" dampened his father's ranch near Oceanside, Hatfield had pleased people in Los Angeles and farmers in the Central and San Joaquin valleys by fulfilling hundreds of their rainmaking contracts.

Binney and the San Diego Wide Awake Improvement Club persisted. Early in December, 1915, a delegation from the club approached Hatfield in his Eagle Rock home outside Los Angeles, asking him if he'd consider showering aid on San Diego by filling the Morena Reservoir with water. He offered to provide rain free, then charge $1,000 per inch for anything between forty and fifty inches. All rain over fifty inches also would be free.

The council, exchanging grins and a few nudges, based its four-to-one vote on a $10,000 flat fee, payable when the reservoir filled up. Hatfield, with help from his younger brother Joel, built a twenty-foot tower base then added an eight-foot extension for his tanks and other paraphenalia next to Morena Dam, sixty miles east of San Diego. Early in the new year, smoke and fumes wafted upward, according to Shelley Higgins.

On January 10 it rained hard. Five days later it poured, and water kept falling for five more days. The downpour temporarily halted a Panama-California Exposition in Balboa Park. Officials scrubbed opening day races at the new Agua Caliente Race Track in Tijuana. Dry river beds filled so fast that some smaller bridges disappeared.

Not everyone believed Hatfield, The Rainmaker, should claim the credit.

"While it obviously is raining hard," said city attorney Terence Cosgrove, "and although obviously the runoff is pouring into the Morena Reservoir, no money should be paid until it is determined that this is the direct result of Mr. Hatfield's efforts."

Rising waters marooned a Santa Fe train just north of the city and sea launches rescued the passengers. More bridges washed away. Homes flooded. Someone at city hall decided this was too much too soon and tried calling Hatfield but the telephone lines were down, according to *Lost Legends of the West,* written by Brad Williams and Choral Pepper.

The saturated soil served as a skidway for the water. A dam at Lower Otay Lake "simply vanished under the pressure" said Williams and Pepper. The Sweetwater Dam ruptured. Muddy waters covered farms and ranches. Homes slipped off their foundations; some ended up like flotsam. Enough water flowed over the dam to have filled the reservoir a second time, Hatfield estimated.

The Hatfield duo headed back toward San Diego and when they saw the extent of the damage began identifying themselves as the Benson brothers in case someone might seek revenge.

Talking with reporters on February 4, Charles Hatfield said he shouldn't be held accountable for damage or for the one dozen or so storm-related fatalities. "I entered into a contract with the city and it was up to the city to take the necessary precautions."

Cosgrove ruled the city should not pay him the $10,000. If it did, flood damage suits would follow. They did anyway: three and a half million dollars worth. Hatfield badgered the city council then offered to settle for $4,000 and even filed a law suit for the money San Diego owed him. Cosgrove countered, saying the city would pay his fee if he'd handle the lawsuits pending against the city for hiring him in the first place. The city ignored him and continued to ignore The Rainmaker's suit until 1938 when it dropped from limbo as a dead issue. In two court cases that came to trial, the rain was deemed an act of God, not Hatfield, said Thomas W. Patterson in the Winter 1970 edition of *The Journal of San Diego History*.

Born in the midwest in 1876, Charles Hatfield came west with the family as a lad and lived in San Diego, Los Angeles, then in San Diego County. His rainmaking attempts came after researching meteorology and the experiments by men who encouraged rain with heat from fires and concussions from explosions. Meanwhile he supported himself as a sewing machine salesman and later as sales manager.

Hatfield's success ratio stemmed from his sense of timing and his weather forecasting skill, not his chemicals, said Stanford University president Dr. David Starr Jordan in a 1925 *Science Magazine* article. Hatfield could sign contracts with people in desperate straits because of drought and pledge precipitation within a few months to a year, knowing his chances ranged from good to excellent, the article said.

The San Diego deluge didn't place Hatfield high and dry on the shelf. What did cause his rainmaking retirement, however, was Boulder Dam, now called Hoover Dam, and irrigation networks across thirsty sections of Southern California.

He switched to a career that remained constant despite the weather — selling sewing machines in Glendale. His secret rainmaking formula died with him in 1958, according to his brother Paul.

Burt Lancaster played a character resembling Charles Hatfield in the 1956 movie *The Rainmaker*, based on a play with the same name. A musical, *110 In The Shade*, also added to the folk hero's fame.

With a handshake, Wilde concludes a border ceremony led by Mexico's General Estabar Cantu about 1910. To Wilde's right is John D. Spreckels.

Wilde so admired Irving Gill's fountain (page 18), now located at Horton Plaza, he had the tower of his house redone to resemble its top after this photo was taken. The house still stands at 24th and Broadway, a street he had renamed from "D."

A mayor who matched his name

Some people believed the ball would be San Diego's social event of a lifetime. Edward, Prince of Wales, the man destined one day to rule England, planned to visit the city in 1920. For his gala welcoming party, members of the city's top society pondered their wardrobes and reviewed their etiquette books. Some of them voiced a concern: "What ever shall we do with the mayor?"

Mayor Louis J. Wilde, in the eyes of the upper crust, was, putting it charitably, unpredictable. The mention of his name created crimson complexions and hiked blood pressures in some parts of town.

Wilde had plunged into politics in 1917 after the city condemned five-and-a-half acres of his ranch. He defeated his opponent, George W. Marston, a department store owner and philanthropist, in a campaign battle of "smokestacks vs. geraniums," as Wilde phrased it.

City councilman Walter Moore once wrote what Wilde took as "a slurring note," so the mayor tracked him down, belted him once, then belted him again, even though Moore towered over him Wilde broke his finger flinging a gavel at another councilman.

Behavior like this kept the city nettled or bemused. So, as the night of the big ball drew closer, some of Mayor Wilde's constituents privately wished their leader might conveniently break a leg or at least severely bruise a lip before the prince arrived on the *H. M. S. Renown.*

No such luck. Wilde's daughter, Lucille, was preparing for her debut, a rite of passage that for some young females serves as notice of their marital availability. Her parents had chosen the posh Hotel del Coronado for the coming out ball. The mayor decided they should combine the ball with the prince's welcoming party.

Out went invitations, addressed by the mayor's wife Frances — and top society waited. And waited. And then realized the mayor's mailing list included mostly his friends, neighbors and cronies. City attorney Shelley J. Higgins was the sole city hall representative invited. Not a single city council member made the list.

If the handsome prince suspected anything, he remained discreet on that April night. One person may have made an impression. Wallis Warfield Simpson attended.   Later, King Edward would relinquish his claim to the throne so he could marry the American, there being a ban in England on royalty marrying commoners. In her autobiography, Simpson maintained they met elsewhere, but San Diegans tended to ignore this, finding it took the edge off their accounts of the evening.

Shelley Higgins thought the ball a smashing success, according to his book *This Amazing City — San Diego*. Higgins never quite understood why Wilde took a liking to him because, as a fledgling assistant city attorney, he represented San Diego in the condemmnation suit against Mayor Wilde in 1916.

Wilde originally set a price of $6,000 for the land the city needed for a small dam, then he reconsidered and lowered the amount by $1,000. Higgins' boss, city attorney Terence B. Cosgrove, felt that was still much too high and declared, "Let's start condemnation proceedings."

The jury and the judge followed standard practice and visited the property. Wilde fed them a sumptious lunch and possible gave them something to slake their thirst. After deliberating, the jury set the property's value at $18,000. Higgins gasped and quickly asked for a new trial, stating the hospitality might have influenced the panel. Instead, the judge suggested halving the award. Higgins agreed.

Not at all appeased, Wilde launched his mayorality campaign, motivated by a vow that he would fire the city hall staff after taking office. The establishment's favorite, George W. Marston, ran on a platform of better city planning, more parks, an improved water front and water conservation. The working class, goaded by Wilde, interpreted this as anti-jobs. The "smokestacks vs. geraniums" slogan worked in 1917 and again two years later when Wilde was reelected.

Born in Iowa City, Iowa, on July 16, 1865, Louis J. Wilde worked as a young man operating an elevator, then selling insurance. He made his fortune investing in Texas oil fields and arrived in San Diego in 1903 where he organized two new banks and presided over two others. Land development and building projects brought in more cash.

When he turned to ranching, Wilde ordered 20,000 silk worms plus some thread spinning machines. The worms, after munching on mulberry leaves, would produce silk. Or so went the theory. They refused to deliver.

True to his campaign promise, one of Wilde's first acts as mayor was to fire Cosgrove. With a characteristically deadpan expression, Cosgrove said, "Sorry, but it becomes my duty, as a legal advisor, to advise you that the power to appoint and remove the city attorney rests with the city council, on which body you as mayor have no vote."

Recalled Higgins: "I thought the mayor's neck would burst."

Wilde did not run for a third time. Instead he moved to Los Angeles. He died there in 1924. For years afterward San Diegans could recall those tempestuous years of his terms in office and say, "Yes, those certainly were the Wilde years."

Sharp pieces of wire, interwoven in his habit, helped Father Serra atone for his sins, including, perhaps, some harsh thoughts he may have harbored about governors he dealt with in Alta California.

Before its 1931 restoration, San Diego Mission looked its years. Father Serra in 1769 established this bottom rung of a ladder of 21 missions that would be built under the leadership of the Franciscan padres.

Father Junipero Serra:
Builder of a ladder in a new world

With a cry of rage the half-stewed English skipper whipped out a knife and place it at Father Junipero Serra's throat. For a moment it appeared the thirty-nine-year-old friar's voyage to New Spain would end only fourteen days away from his native Mediterranean island of Majorca. The captain, however, stalked off for another snort, still furious with this five-foot, three-inch priest. The reason? Father Serra had politely refuted the captain's erroneous theological statements, correcting them by citing chapter and verse from memory.

This was the first of many miraculous escapes for the padre, a man destined to build a ladder of missions in Alta (Upper) California. Here he would introduce Christianity and basic facets of European civilization. The presidios, or garrison towns, near the missions would, according to the plan, achieve the primary goal of Spain's ruler, King Carlos III: to inhibit the Russians and British from coastal inroads, at least for a time.

On Father Serra's next leg of the voyage—from Cadiz to Puerto Rico—the ship's captain rationed drinking water. Then when almost within sight of Vera Cruz, a storm hit. By dusk the alarmed sailors begged their captain, "Run the ship aground so at least some lives will be saved." But by morning, on December 6, 1749, the winds subsided. The padre, after ninety-nine days at sea, noted he had not been seasick once.

From Vera Cruz, he chose the Franciscan tradition and set off on foot toward Mexico City two-hundred and fifty miles away. An Andalusian friar joined him. Neither of them owned a peso. On this and later journeys the indomitable Serra:

Survived a communion at which someone poisoned the wine.

Enjoyed food and shelter provided by an elderly couple and their grandson in an area where the natives swore no one lived.

Out of the blue was granted shelter during a night when the temperature unexpectedly zoomed below freezing.

Ignored heat and flies and evaded snakes and alligators on his rounds among Indians in Mexico where he spent his first seventeen years on the continent.

As mosts priests did then, Father Serra imitated various saints during his services. He lowered his gray habit to his waist and lashed himself or beat his chest with a jagged rock or burned his flesh with flame of a taper. Sharp pieces of wire interwoven in his sackcloth garment went next to his skin. The pain atoned for "my own imperfections and sins, as well as the sins of others," he said.

At the age of fifty-five he became *padre-presidente* of the missions planned for Alta California. On the trip northward he was nearly forced to turn back because of an ulcerated foot and leg, caused nearly seventeen years earlier by an insect bite that had refused to heal, but had been accepted, even welcomed by him as another form of penance. A protesting muleteer, at the priest's insistence, applied the same kind of poultice on the friar as he used on mules. The next morning the bouncy patient felt so much better he called it a miracle.

On July 1, 1769 he and his group arrived in San Diego. He found an advance sea-faring party decimated by scurvy and low on provisions. Captain Gaspar de Portolá mustered the men still on their feet and struggled north, as ordered, toward Monterey. A handful of sailors headed back on the *San Antonio* for supplies and reinforcments.

Serra remained with two other padres, Dr. Pedro Prat, four soldiers, forty Baja Indians and the ailing sailors. As Don J. Baxter described it in *Missions of California*, "By a slender thread, California was formally tied to Spain."

The local Indians first greeted the newcomers by signs, then tested them with a surprise attack. The soldiers' fire power, meager as it was, nonetheless gained respect.

By the time Portolá's party returned, food had almost run out. "March 19 will be the date of the feast of St. Joseph," Portolá told Father Serra. "If a ship does not arrive by then, my men and I will return to Baja."

The thought of surrendering this toehold hit the padre hard. As the date approached, the entire assembly joined in a novena of prayers to Saint Joseph, the expedition's patron saint. On the afternoon of March 19 as the soldiers packed, a lookout sighted the *San Antonio's* sails in the distance.

Father Serra celebrated High Mass every month the rest of his life on March 19.

He next established Mission San Carlos Borromeo de Carmelo in Monterey. These busy days introduced the biggest cross to bear — dealing with military-civil authorities. Pedro Fages, after assuming his post as commandante, tried covering his inexperience by tough discipline, which only succeeded in infuriating his men. His ambition found him wielding more power over the padres and missions than his orders warranted. His rigidity created friction at a time when it could take years for a reply to a Mexico City message.

Fed up, the padre himself headed for Mexico City, convinced he must describe in person the plight of the missions. The rugged journey nearly killed him, but he found an ally in Viceroy Chevalier Antonio Maria Bucareli. Soon Fages was transferred.

In no time at all his replacement, Don Fernando de Rivera, placed roadblocks before new mission development, citing a scarcity of troops and supplies. When Monterey became the new capital of the upper and lower Californias in 1776, Don Felipe de Neve became the governor. Rivera left for Baja California. Neve, historians agree, proved a good administrator, but his bureaucratic rules nonetheless became another thorn in Father Serra's side.

For three years Neve blocked Serra's right to confirm his "dear children," the Indians. Through it all, the padre maintained his dignity. To other priests he confessed, "I feel hogtied." The issue ended in 1781, and he began confirming the Indians. Three years later he died at the age of seventy. He was buried at the Carmel Mission.

One major accomplishment came after visiting Bucareli, who told the *padre-presidente*, "Put into writing your petitions on behalf of your beloved Indians and solutions to problems we have discussed." The resulting *Representacion* became the foundation for the first major law in California. According to Don DeNevi and Noel Francis Moholy in their book *Junipero Serra*, it became a "Bill of Rights" for Indians that "would affect the military, post office officials, missionaries, colonists, the college and even the Council of the Indies in Spain."

Father Junipero Serra was elected a candiate for canonization as a saint in 1934. In 1985, Pope John Paul II declared him "venerable," which, observers say, is the most difficult step in having the Vatican elevate someone to sainthood, and during his September, 1987 visit to California was expected to beatify Father Serra. This would virtually clinch the padre's selection and make him the state's first saint.

Father Anthony D. Ubach:
The poet who became a padre

A pounding on the door awakened Father Anthony Domenic Ubach in the middle of the night. When he opened it a rancher from Mission Valley exclaimed, "Can you come at once, padre? My daughter has seen the ghost again and this time she says it harmed her." The priest gathered some materials, grabbed a cigar and hitched his horse to the carriage. He followed the rancher four or five miles northward until they reached the ranch house where the priest performed the exorcism rites. A few weeks later on his way to minister among the Indians he learned the ghost had disappeared.

This 1878 ghost busting victory stands as one of the few that the padre could claim on the outer edges of San Diego where many of the Indians lived. Time after time this champion of justice for the Indians witnessed deceit, broken vows and indifference by the United States government and the recently arrived settlers. The Indians, rightful heirs to portions of the mission lands, were booted out by squatters, killed upon slight provocation and routinely disfranchised, despised and deceived.

The discouraged priest found hope with the arrival of Helen Hunt Jackson. She came on assignment in 1881 for a series of magazine articles about the mission Indians and he showed her around the county where she saw the squalor, the illness and the prejudice. The articles, later published in the book *A Century of Dishonor*, cited case after case of government disregard for Indians' rights. But Congress, as it frequently did on this matter, only took it under advisement. Jackson reached a far larger audience with *Ramona*, a romance novel that dramatized injustices to Indians. Again, however, only a few corrective steps followed.

One hero in the novel, Father Gaspara, closely resembled Father

Conducting services for 47 of the 60 sailors who died in a 1905 explosion aboard the U.S.S. Bennington is Father Antonio Ubach, left. Two of the four boilers blew up on July 21 while the ship was anchored in San Diego Bay.

Ubach. Later he admitted Jackson's description of him was on target. She wrote: "He had a nature at once fiery and poetic and there were three things he could have been — a soldier, a poet or a priest."

The son of distinguished Barcelona, Spain, parents, he had indeed impressed people with his poetry, scholarship and his skill as a swordsman. His beard, allowed by church officials through special dispensation, covered a scar inflicted by an opponent, according to persistent rumors.

"The look of the soldier he had never quite lost — neither the look nor the tread; and his flashing dark eyes, heavy black beard and hair, and quick elastic step, seemed sometimes strangely out of harmony with his priest's gown," Jackson declared about her fictional priest, omitting the ever-present cigar her real-life model carried.

She also wrote, "And it was the sensitive soul of the poet in him which had made him withdraw himself more and more, year after year, as he found himself comparitively powerless to do anything for the hundreds of Indians."

Father Ubach began making his rounds in Indian territory a few days after arriving in San Diego in 1866. A few slapdash frame buildings clustered around Presidio Hill, and small adobe buildings with splotchy whitewashed walls greeted a vistor's eye then. The population stood at about 2,000. He rode his wagon on his tribal visits, often sleeping on the ground at night by a small fire and, like his friends, dining on acorns and plants, undeterred by his asthma and other health problems.

The padre's parishoners laid the cornerstone for a church in Old Town on July 18, 1869, one century after Father Junipero Serra's groundbreaking for California's first mission less than a mile away. But by the time the church walls hit eye level, people had virtually deserted Old Town. Everyone moved into the Horton Addition. Alonzo Horton, a shrewd promoter, donated two of his lots to the Catholic Church and members raised money with benefits and concerts for their new worship place.

One of Father Ubach's projects succeeded, to a degree. After countless letters and appeals, he obtained government backing for an Industrial Boarding School for Indian children, but funds never matched the needs, so he kept trying to cope with debts until government funding stopped altogether.

He struggled with the Indians' problems and confronted the challenges of a city variously infested with gamblers, prostitutes, boozers, con men, robbers, no-accounts and shady politicians. Real estate booms caused even devout parishoners and other men of the cloth to forget First Timothy 1:10. The busts that followed the booms caused lamentations.

Father Anthony Ubach died in 1907. Ten years later a new church building rose atop the long neglected 1869 foundation in Old Town. The original San Diego Mission was restored in 1931. The abandoned industrial school became an orphanage. And the lawlessness and boom-and-bust cycles moderated, even as justice of a sort helped the plight of the dwindling number of Indians.

Father Ubach's days were spent in ways that gave flesh to the words of another poet, William Wordsworth:

"That best portion of a good man's life,
His little, nameless, unremembered acts
Of kindness and love."

A former farm hand and teacher, the wiry Rector Henry Restarick exhibited a sense of humor during his 20-year ministry at St. Paul's Episcopal Church.

Henry B. Restarick:
A rector who believed in action

Banks closed their doors, businesses folded and San Diego became a magnet for the destitute in the panic of 1893. Hoboes and tramps converged on the city, joining hundreds of unemployed residents in a struggle for survival.

Henry Bond Restarick, rector of St. Paul's Episcopal Church, thought of a plan. The Keating family had donated an old house, destined one day for use as a hospital, but now it stood empty. Reverend Restarick scrounged thirty cots and hired a cook esteemed for his wholesome stew recipe. "I had a large number of tickets printed which were sold to townspeople ten for a dollar," he said in *My Personal Recollections*. "When tramps approached, they got a ticket and received a free meal and bed." To help offset expenses, the rector wangled donations of wood from owners of a harbor wharf being torn down. The men split, sawed, then sold it as kindling.

County constables received a mileage fee for apprehending tramps and bringing them to San Diego. The rector discovered the same tramps showing up regularly, brought back by the law enforcers who pocketed sizeable amounts of the taxpayers' money. After he pointed out the racket, authorities halted it.

This sort of direct action characterized the reverend's twenty-year ministry at the church, which originally was named Holy Trinity until 1885, three years after his arrival at the age of twenty-seven.

He came from Iowa, frail from malaria-induced digestive problems. When he had applied for the parish, he was still single. Some of his new flock wondered if an unmarried member might snag him. On a day when he was scheduled to perform a wedding, he first made a call on a young lady. He chatted a bit, then stood up, saying, "I must go for I am going to marry someone." She reacted with a look of disappointment, "What, so soon?" After an awkward moment, the blushing rector said he had just married the month before. His wife May joined him as quickly as he could rent an old house.

His first communion service attracted six women and one man in a frame building capable of holding perhaps one-hundred people, if solidly packed. In two decades church membership would reach more than four-hundred, making it one of the most dynamic and prosperous in the West.

In the early days, W. W. Bowser, brother-in-law of promoter Alonzo E. Horton, concocted a membership building ploy. He would approach, say, six Methodists and declare, "If you'll come with me next Sunday to hear my minister, I'll go with you the following Sunday to hear yours." When the rector asked about this strategy, Bowser replied, "Well, if I have to go with them, I got six for one." As for the Methodist minister's sermon, Bowser said, "It was all right for ten minutes and after that it was dribblings." The rector thus concluded, "It was better to stop after one had said all he knew on a subject than to fill in time with poor stuff."

The Restaricks' small house at Twelfth and A streets rented for twenty dollars a month, which, on a monthly salary of seventy-five dollars, seemed stiff. Thanks, however, to dining-out invitations and thoughtful people who sent "delicacies," they were able to open a savings account.

About the only cloud over the rector's happy childhood in England had been the shortage of money. His father had endorsed a note for a brother whose business failed, so years of penny pinching followed. The lad had to promise his father he would never endorse a note, and this, the rector said, saved him many headaches over the years.

His mother read Dickens aloud to the family at night, imbuing the boy with a love of books and reading. His father, a devout, open-minded man, loved a good joke, a quality the son inherited. Looking back on those days, the Reverend Restarick recognized that his main fault was a quick temper and "Like most people with

First service in the new St. Paul's church at Eighth and C took place on Easter Day, 1887. A predecessor church was named Holy Trinity.

that failing I showed that side of my disposition to those I loved the best."

He emigrated to Canada at the age of seventeen, then sought opportunity in America, toiling from daybreak to dark as a farm laborer in Nebraska and Iowa. He worked his way through college and was ordained in Davenport. The years in San Diego were among his happiest. He became friends with with Father Anthony Ubach, the last of the old mission priests, partly because of a mutual interest in helping Indians.

These two, it seemed to the rector, were the only people who did not buy and sell property in the land boom of the mid-Eighties. On paper, the rector's servant was worth $18,000 at one point and a church alderman on one lot alone was worth $60,000. Both of them ignored the Reverend Restarick's urgings to sell. Like thousands of other speculators, including many clergymen, they ended up broke and left town when the "debacle" came in 1888.

On Sundays the wiry rector officiated at three and sometimes four services. These included St. Paul's missions within range of a horseback ride. "I considered all of San Diego County as my parish," he said. He trained men in the reading of the services and the sermon and they led worship in as many as ten missions sponsored by St. Paul's in the area. The hierarchy was so impressed they asked him to write a book about the Lay Readers Association.

A friend once told him how he handled the awkward moment after the wedding ceremony when the bridgroom asks, "How much do I owe you?" So the rector used his friend's line, "That depends on the value you place on the bride," with a miner who had struck it rich in Arizona. The rector held out his hand. After four twenty-dollar gold pieces plopped into it, the miner asked, "How long are you going to hold out your hand?" The reply: "Just so long as you continue to drop twenty dollar gold pieces into it." The miner dropped one more and said, "I guess I'll quit." The line continued to work, but the rector finally dropped it after one groom gave him fifty cents.

When a parishoner proposed a fair as a fund raiser, the Reverend Restarick vetoed the idea. "Fairs are hard on the women, who not only do all the work but often contribute most of the money, buying things they do not need," he said. Bazaars were different. At least they were in those days, because they enabled local talent to perform, and the rector, who loved attending the theater any time he visited San Francisco, preferred amateur talent to none at all.

In 1902 he became the first Episcopal bishop of Hawaii where his knack for innovation and inspiration continued until his retirement in 1920. He died in Honolulu in 1933.

Captain M. Dustin:
An officer and a soul searcher

In battles for the souls of wayward San Diegans, Salvation Army Captain M. Dustin and her troops faced risks. Heckling, threats and near riots hampered their campaigns. Elsewhere in the West, three of the Army's workers were murdered. The first Salvation Army hall in Sacramento was burned down. Officers in Los Angeles were shot at.

Captain Dustin didn't experience action that intense. She served in San Diego just four months through November 1888, but the organization did find resistance in establishing a beachhead. The branch had officially opened the previous year on March 31, but an advance guard had gained a toehold of sorts after New Year's Day in 1887.

"A sort of bobtailed Salvation Army held a meeting on the corner of Fifth and E streets last evening," the *San Diego Union* reported on January 7. "The band, which a week ago paraded twenty-two strong, now shows up but six, the coldness of the evenings having dampened somewhat their enthusiastic ardor to convert the world and do it suddenly."

Captain Dustin came West at the age of twenty-one after the

death of first her mother, then a sister. California relatives had invited her to join them. "In the midst of new scenes my mind was turned away from seeking the Saviour," she admitted in an auto-biographical sketch in *The War Cry*, a Salvation Army newspaper. "At the end of six months, I firmly believe, I was led by God into the Salvation Army barracks at Oakland." The fact that its workers were undergoing persecution and looked down on "made no difference to me," she stated.

In her brief stay in San Diego, the *Union* reported on two more incidents, the first being a September 24 summary of a city council meeting:

"John Mack, proprietor of a boarding-house on Seventh street between F and G, presented a petition in which he declared that he had lost seventeen lodgers, and that others were threatening to leave his place, on account of the 'very noisy and uproarious conduct' of the salvation army, which holds its meetings in the old Baptist church adjoining his property."

Then a week later:

THE SALVATION ARMY
An Out-door Meeting Broken Up Last Evening

A crowd of roughs gathered around George D. Mealy of the United States branch of the salvation army, and a follower named Luther T. Dennis, who were holding an open-air service on the corner of Fifth and E streets last night, and became so demonstrative with yells and curses that the evangelists were compelled to beat a retreat. They made for the holiness tent, at the corner of D and Sixth streets, and were followed by the crowd, which by this time numbered over 500 persons of all classes, many of whom took up the cause of the salvationists. The entire crowd surrounded the tent, and for a moment it looked as if a general melee would ensue, but Deputy Chief Barton arrived on the scene, and without much trouble quelled the disturbance and cleared the tent.

A group of toughs on October 4 using "Loud and extremely unparliamentary language" interrupted the Army's meeting until police showed up.

Reactions like these were not unusual in the West, according to Edward H. McKinley, a Salvation Army officer and an associate

Despite taunts, near-riots and threats, Captain M. Dustin led Salvation Army activities in 1888 "to convert the world and do it suddenly," as a San Diego Union *reporter phrased it.*

World War I brought Salvation Army and Elks Club teamwork in San Diego. The Army's assistance during the war and in natural disasters led to an over-subscribed $13 million U.S. fund raising drive after the end of hostilities.

history professor at Asbury College in Wilmore, Kentucky. "Many people in those raw, unsettled times were overtly hostile to religion," he said. "Physical violence, ranging from missiles to actual blows, rained down on the pioneers. The Army officially declared in 1884 that 'the extreme godlessness of most of the population on the Pacific Coast makes the task of our officers there one of extraordinary difficulty.'"

On a warm August night in 1889 three Army women were jailed in San Diego on the charge of being a nuisance. Their tambourine playing and singing disturbed the peace, said the arresting officer. An unnamed woman posted bail the same night and the charge was dismissed the next week.

On March 6, 1890, almost ten years to the day since the Salvation Army began in the United States and twenty-five years after its origin in England, the *San Diego Union* reported: "The Salvation Army and its big bass drum caused two horses to run away yesterday, and nearly cost one lady her life. When her horse took fright at the uncanny sound of the drum she was thrown out of her carriage and was badly bruised and had her nose broken. Earlier in the day another runaway was caused by the startling noise. Complaints are made daily about the disaster caused by the Army and its drum, yet nothing can be done to abate the nuisance."

But things have a way of ending happily in San Diego. Here's an item from the *Union's* September 10, 1891 edition: "The Salvation Army attracted great attention last night by reason of a full brass band, lately imported from the north, which discoursed religious music in much better time and tune than usual."

Salvation Army records do not reveal what became of Captain Dustin. The emphasis on the organization's mission rather than the individuals who make it happen probably would suit her just fine.

The Explorers

Juan Rodriguez Cabrillo:
The almost forgotten explorer

"**He failed.** That expedition proved worthless." These were the reactions that almost made Juan Rodriguez Cabrillo's California coast expedition in 1542 a forgotten saga. News of the journey had created no stir. The value of the California region was regarded as marginal in Spain and Mexico.

Cabrillo didn't find the Strait of Anian, the mythical link between the Pacific with the Atlantic Ocean, which the English called the Northwest Passage. He didn't connect with China or the route to the Spice Islands. He found no gold. In fact, he died before completing his expedition, the victim of an infected broken arm or, according to some accounts, a broken leg.

He did accomplish, however, the discovery of San Diego Bay. Not only did he find the bay, he achieved the nearly impossible task of building his flagship the *San Salvadore* and a dozen other ships in the torrid climate of Central America using unskilled Indian labor. During his journey he charted important points along the California coast that guided later explorers.

The sketchy details of Cabrillo's life arouse some speculation. He probably was born in Portugal and acquired navigating skills as a captain with her navy until joining land forces that in 1519 challenged Hernán Cortés' conquistadores in Mexico, and lost. Cabrillo, about 29 then, allied himself with Cortés in the bloody, often ruthless conquest of the Aztecs. He was wounded, once under Cortés' command and again while serving under Pedro de Alvarado during the attempted annihilation of the Quiché Indians in Guatamala. His courage and know-how earned a promotion to captain of bowmen. As a reward for his soldiering, Cabrillo received property near present day Guatamala City, then traveled to Spain for an arranged marriage.

He " . . . returned to settle down and become a man of property and considerable influence," observed Richard F. Pourade in *The Explorers*, the first of six volumes on San Diego's history. In 1536 Alvarado chose Cabrillo as chief of an ambitious undertaking: construction of a navy. Half of the ships would explore for islands of the South Sea, as the Pacific Ocean was called, and the others would probe along the Alta (Upper) California coast. The Guatamala forests offered ample wood, but in the summer the heat was so intense work could only proceed between midnight and dawn.

For four arduous years with Indian slaves as his ship builders, Cabrillo perservered. The navy he launched included three galleons, each with a displacement of 200 tons, seven ships of 100 tons and three small vessels. Instruments, metalwork and anchors came from Spain where budget department pencil pushers concluded eighty ships could have been built for the same amount of money spent in Guatamala for thirteen vessels.

Cabrillo himself invested in the navy. He not only captained the *San Salvadore*, he owned it, and thus would have merited a share in the rewards of treasure found or passageways revealed. As the navy's admiral, he commanded 1,000 officers and seamen, but most of them lacked know-how or training. The armada anchored at Navidad, Mexico, near the present day city of Manzanillo. Then Alvarado died in a skirmish with Indians and Mexico's viceroy authorized Cabrillo to proceed with the expedition aboard the *San Salvadore*, accompanied by the *Victoria*. They sailed on June 27, 1542. Buffeted by strong head winds, the ships made a scant 20 miles or so by day and anchored at night. It must have seemed they traveled sideways on some days. At Ensenada in mid-September the explorers spent five days, then on September 28 Point Loma was sighted.

A summary of chief pilot Bartolome Ferrer's journal, written in the third person, stated: "On the following Thursday they went

F. GERITZ

Juan Rodríguez Cabrillo

Cabrillo named his Alta California discovery San Miguel, but Vizcaino, as he frequently did, changed names — in this case, to San Diego.

San Diego Bay, as Cabrillo and his crew probably saw it in 1542, is shown in a diorama at the Cabrillo National Monument on Point Loma.

about six leagues along a coast running north-northwest, and discovered a port, closed and very good, which they named San Miguel . . . Having cast anchor in it, they went ashore where there were people. Three of them waited, but all the rest fled. To these three they gave some presents and they said by signs that in the interior men like the Spaniards had passed. They gave signs of great fear. On the night of this day they went ashore from the ships to fish with a net, and it appears that there were some Indians and they began to shoot at them with arrows and wounded three men." Cabrillo wisely decided not to counter-attack. He learned the next day that the "interior men like the Spaniards" had killed a number of the Indians. The intruders likely were part of the land expedition which neared the Colorado River two years earlier under the leadership of Francisco Vásquez de Coronado.

The ships left the port now known as San Diego six days later and touched base at Catalina Island, San Pedro and Santa Monica. Several stops were made along the Santa Barbara Channel. At La Posesión Island, which today is called San Miguel Island, the admiral fell and injured himself. Nonetheless, the intrepid explorer led the ships north of San Francisco until storms forced them back to the island where he had fallen. He died there January 3, 1543. He had passed command to Ferrer, charging him to continue with the exploration.

Historian Richard Pourade describes San Miguel Island as a " . . . barren, treeless, windswept mesa beset by some of the roughest currents of the California coast." It seems an appropriate resting place for the rugged Cabrillo. The grave of this almost forgotten explorer never has been found. Despite the long neglect, Cabrillo finally achieved distinction as a leader with courage, wisdom and a dedication to duty.

Sebastián Vizcaíno:
The best of the map makers

Spain's viceroy, Gaspar de Zuniga y Acevedo, Conde de Monterey, faced a problem. He knew the expedition to chart California's coast should be launched soon because the presence of first English and then Dutch ships threatened Spain's control of the Pacific Ocean. If the expedition could find new ports they would provide haven for the repair of ships shuttling from Manila to Acapulco in New Spain. Then military vessels could accompany the heavily laden galleons, furnishing protection from pirates. Monterey was impatient because storms already had delayed the three ships scheduled for the California reconaissance under the command of Sebastián Vizcaíno.

"We still need fifty to sixty more seamen," he was informed.

Mariners just were not interested. The hazards of extended sea duty had caused fifty of Vizcaíno's men to desert at Mazatlán on his first expedition. Ships in those days were about the size of a tennis court so severe storms often exacted a terrible toll. Invariably, voyages lasting more than three or four months brought the telltale, painful scurvy symptoms — bleeding underneath the skin, loss of strength, bleeding gums. The mariners' diet of beef jerky, salt pork, dried beans, garbonzos and hardtack lacked the fresh fruits and vegetables that would have prevented the illness. Fog, sometimes hostile Indians, the unpredictability of finding fresh water or bartering for food with the natives — all gave seamen pause.

After learning that more men were needed, the viceroy came up with an idea. One can imagine how he phrased it: "Very well, find me some *soldiers* who've had sea duty. I'll sign them on."

This plan worked, but only after he raised the enlistment pay from fifteen to eighteen pesos, according to the book *Vizcaíno* by W. Michael Mathes.

Thus, Vizcaíno finally set sail from Acapulco May 5, 1602 with a full complement of men for his flagship, the *San Diego*, a former Peruvian galleon the *Santo Tomas* and the frigate *Tres Reyes*. With frequent stops for map making and searches for food, wood and water, on November 10 the ships anchored at Bahia de San Miguel, which Rodriguez Cabrillo discovered and named in 1542. Vizcaíno, as he did with most of his stopping points, renamed the bay. He called it San Diego in honor of the flagship's patron saint.

A landing party discovered abundant water, game and firewood while other crew members began repairing the ships. Indians at a nearby rancheria gave the visitors rabbit and squirrel pelts. On their ninth day, Vizcaíno called his top officers in for a council, the Spanish equivalent of a board of directors session, and they voted for a departure the next day. The *Tres Reyes* led the way as they edged up the coast, the cartographers busy sketching during limited hours of daylight. When the three ships anchored in Monterey Bay, Vizcaíno thought he had found the ideal port Spain needed.

It had been spotted seven years earlier by Sebastián Rodriguez Cermaño, who named it San Pedro, but Vizcaíno is credited with its discovery. He renamed it Monterey Bay in honor of the viceroy. At another council, officers decided to send the *Santo Tomas* back to New Spain with 40 crewmen ill with scurvy. By then, sixteen men had died from it. The other two boats continued northward, reaching Mendocino Cape before storms and spreading illness forced a turnabout.

Historians disagree about the value of Vizcaíno's expedition. The discovery of Monterey Bay proved a major find, but its harbor didn't compare with San Diego or San Francisco. Still it served for the smaller ships of that day.

Seagoers used the maps from Vizcaíno's voyages through the end of the 18th Century even though Spain largely ignored them and the information he'd accumulated until the Portolá-Serra expedition 167 years later. Mapmakers continued grappling with the

Merchant-adventurer Vizcaino deserves credit for urging the settlement of California, as well as for his maps, says his biographer W. Michael Mathes.

persistent myth of a Strait of Anian (the British called it the Northwest Passage) connecting with the Atlantic Ocean, and two of Vizcaíno's officers helped perpetuate the idea. And, lastly, with frequently favorable breezes behind them, the Spanish ships heading south enroute to Acapulco along the California coast rarely needed layovers.

Nonetheless, Vizcaíno deserves a prominent place among the world's explorers, Mathes believes, because of his unmatched knowledge of Alta (Upper) and Baja California and because, "None of Vizcaíno's predeccesors urged so strongly the settlement of California, nor contributed more permanently to its cartography."

The wonder of it all is that the merchant-adventurer even ventured forth after first attempting a similar expedition five years earlier. Born in 1548, he grew up learning the arts of land-based warfare and took part in the invasion of Portugal. After three years of adventuring in New Spain he sailed in 1586 to Manila, which Spain controlled as a pivotal point in her trade with the Orient.

Vizcaíno became a successful merchant, then returned to New Spain where he and his partners obtained a license for pearl fishing rights off the California coast. His partners reneged, he was arrested for complicity in what authorities first thought was a fraud, then released. During the voyage, part of his crew deserted. More than half of a settlement at La Paz burned down. Following an Indian attack on a land party, nineteen of the armor-clad crew drowned in their attempt to reach the ship. A leaking keel, broken rudder controls and a fierce storm finally forced his return to New Spain.

The earlier journey proved all the more harrowing because Vizcaíno's seven-year-old son Juan had accompanied him.

In his later years, Vizcaíno, promoted to general, vanquished some Dutch invaders and accepted as a reward the job of Acapulco alcalde, or mayor. He died at the age of seventy-eight.

Jedediah Smith:
A trapper who blazed new trails

G overnor-General Jose Maria Echendía was stalling. His inde-
cision resulted from the presence at the San Diego presidio of
Jedediah Smith. The American said that he and his band of five
mountain men had ventured south from the Great Salt Lake into
Mojave country, then west across the desert into the San Bernardino Valley; first in search of beaver, then for survival.

But Echeandía wondered if this lean, six-foot, twenty-seven-
year-old intruder actually might be on a military mission. Beaver
trappers were a new breed, so new, in fact, Echeandía booked
Smith as a *pescadore*— fisherman.

Smith himself feared he would be sent to Echeandía's superiors
in Mexico. He worried not for his personal safety but for the time
lost in getting to the spring hunt. Finally, his papers were
authenticated.

"You may return to your country, but only by the route by which
you came," Echeandía said.

So Jedediah Strong Smith, who ranks behind only Lewis and
Clark for explorations of the American West, continued his journey. Besides opening the first overland pathway to California, he

was the first to cross the Sierra Nevada to the east and the first to reach Oregon by a journey up the California coast.

He became a mountaineer when he was twenty-three, "a mild and Christian man," as one trapper described him. With little more than his rifle and a Bible, he had joined the fur trading company of William H. Ashley in St. Louis. In just three years, Smith's courage, leadership and intelligence earned him a senior partnership. The traits also earned him the respectful sobriquet "Old Jed" from the tough, "ring-tailed screamers" — mountain men whose reputation for brawling, drinking and swearing overshadowed at first the significance of their trailblazing of an unknown land.

After leaving San Diego, Smith did not retrace his route. He led his men back toward the Mojave Desert, then veered north to the San Joaquin Valley and up as far as the American River.

They set their traps and by May 1827, their horses were laden with 1,500 pounds of beaver. But the deep snow of the Sierra blocked the return to the trappers' annual rendezvous near the Great Salt Lake. Smith left most of his party at a camp near the Stanislaus River to look after the furs. Taking two men, seven horses and two mules, he headed up the north fork of the Stanislaus in the general region of what is now known as Ebbetts Pass. They crossed the mountains in just eight days, the first white men to do so, but nearly died of thirst in the "Great Sandy Plain," as he called the Great Basin between the Sierra and the Great Salt Lake, before reaching the rendezvous.

On a return trip to California along the way that later would become known as the Gila Trail, half of Smith's party of 18 men were killed in a surprise attack by Mojave Indians. Once again he came to San Diego, but this time as a prisoner. He was promptly jailed, then released because an American sea captain intervened. "Leave now and never come back," Smith was told. He agreed, but instead of going east he headed up to the Sacramento Valley and met the men he'd left behind the previous year. In the summer of 1826 the party turned toward the Pacific, and journeyed north over and around the heavily timbered coastal hills and up the coastline.

A mountaineer and trapper at the age of 23, the Bible-carrying Jedediah Smith impressed compadres with his know-how and as a "mild and Christian man."

When they reached the Umpqua River, well into Oregon Territory, Indians attacked and Smith was one of the few to escape.

Eventually he made his way back to St. Louis where he sent most of his fur trade earnings to his family. In 1831, on the Santa Fe Trail, Smith scouted for water in advance of a new group of men. He died there at the age of 33 fighting a small band of Comanches.

"He entered the West when it was still largely an unknown land; when he left the mountains, the whole country had been printed on the living maps of his trappers' minds," said author Dale L. Morgan.

James Ohio Pattie:
The imaginative trapper

Creator of the first western potboiler.
This is just one of James Ohio Pattie's claims to fame. A man with a vivid imagination but a flawed memory, he dictated the story of his life to Timothy Flint, who himself knew how to garnish a tale. *The Personal Narrative of James O. Pattie of Kentucky* includes accounts of hair-raising Indian battles, desert hardships, the sympathy of a beautiful young woman, a trumped up jail stay and an incredible medical maneuver during a smallpox epidemic. The book endures despite its exaggerations; there's enough verifiable action to earn a place in historical annals.

His hosts gave Pattie a rude introduction to San Diego in March, 1828. Governor Jose Maria de Echeandía eyed the sorry looking party of eight Americans standing before him and demanded the reason for their California intrusion. James' father, the wiry Sylvester Pattie from Kentucky and Missouri, told the governor how the band of trappers had crossed the desert as a last resort, the sole means of staying alive. All they asked was enough food, gear and horses for a return trip.

That's exactly what trapper Jedediah Smith had asked a year earlier, the governor recalled. Then, after receiving aid, Smith broke his word and headed north instead of east, collecting beaver pelts along the way. Echeandía decided this group had been sent to spy for the Spaniards who, he believed, still coveted California, notwithstanding Mexico's recently won independence. "To the guardhouse with them all," he barked at the guardsmen.

Cut from the mold of a frontiersman, James Ohio Pattie found prison more difficult than fighting Indians, close calls with grizzlies and a parched throat amid the desert. The confinement and illness killed his father. Fighting off his despair, James resolved to regain his freedom.

The jailhouse sergeant brought his sister on a visit. Pattie described her as "a young lady of great personal beauty." In his journal he calls her "Miss Peak," possibly a version of "Pico," says Stanton A. Coblentz in his book *The Swallowing Wilderness*. The Pico family, prominent in Southern California, included Pio Pico who would become governor of California one day.

Miss Peak told the twenty-four-year-old prisoner she would plead his case with the governor. Soon Pattie received a new outfit and shed his rags. His strength returned as meals improved.

A battle of wills ensued between Echeandía and the hot-tempered Pattie, who agreed to translate some documents, then changed his mind. The trapper "was a self-conceited and quick-tempered youth with a freedom of speech that amounted to insolence," according to historian Hubert H. Bancroft.

In the northern part of California a smallpox epidemic erupted. The governor discovered Sylvester Pattie's effects included some vaccine, so he offered James compensation and a year's passport if he would inoculate as many Californians as possible. Pattie agreed, but on the condition of a personal session with the governor and freedom for his fellow Americans. The governor balked until news of additional smallpox deaths produced a face-saving compromise.

Pattie vaccinated nearly 22,000 Mexicans, missionaries, Indians and settlers from other national origins between San Diego and Fort Ross, just north of today's San Francisco, between mid-January and July. He had learned the inoculation technique from his father. People dubbed him the "Magic Man," an apt sobriquet when one seeks the source of all that vaccine. It seems likely the feat owes much to the placebo effect.

At Mission San Francisco de Asis, popularly known now as Mission Delores, the local padre offered Pattie his pay, based on the number of needlings, of five-hundred cows and five-hundred mules plus land enough for their grazing, providing he join the Catholic Church and become a Mexican citizen.

Pattie, ever the patriot, said he could not reply: "My anger choked me."

At Monterey he joined Joaquin Solis' revolt against Governor Eacheandía. After a Solis threat to expel all Americans, Pattie switched allegiances. He helped crush the revolution. The grateful governor offered him a piece of the action if he would remain in California and renounce his American citizenship. "Never!" said Pattie.

He obtained a passport to Mexico City and gained an audience with top officials. His goal: to obtain payment for his San Diego imprisonment and for the furs lost by the trappers. He did not, however, press the case. Pattie sailed to New Orleans, arriving in August, 1830, six years after he and his father headed West. His book came out a year later.

One historian calls it "an epic saga."

Popular hero John C. Frémont, right, did not blaze new trails on his westward expeditions, critics said, but left that up to guides like his friend Kit Carson.

John Charles Frémont:
Impetuous pathfinder

Bivouacked with his rag-tag troops near Point San Pedro, John Charles Frémont saw a small boat approaching land. Four men were on board. He turned to his guide Kit Carson and told him to engage the enemy.

"You mean . . . take those men prisoners?"

Frémont drew himself up to his full five-foot, seven-inch height and said, "I have no room for prisoners."

So Carson and three of the buckskin-clad members of the California Battalion rode their horses close to the shore, dismounted and shot an old man and two young twin brothers as they climbed from the boat. The fourth man escaped. These unarmed Californians were on the way to the San Francisco de Asis Mission, better known today as Delores Mission.

Frémont's impetuosity and penchant for picking a fight were not seen as unusual by the American military men, frontiersmen and settlers seeking action in the early days of the 1846-48 war with Mexico. In California their battles had been few and fleeting.

As a lieutenant in the United States Topographical Corps, Frémont late in 1845 headed west from Washington D. C. on an "exploratory" expedition. Along the way he rounded up sixty sharpshooters, making the party a most unusual looking survey group. Fremont's father-in-law, the powerful Senator Thomas Hart Benton, and Navy Secretary George Bancroft, both expansionist advocates, had privately encouraged the do-it-yourself army. They believed war was imminent and held the view Mexico might cede California to Great Britain.

Senseless shootings and an unauthorized armed force ranked as only two of the unpredictable facets of a man the United States public now hailed as the Pathfinder for his two earlier expeditions. They produced maps and descriptions that began opening the gates to a land of rich promise.

Upon their arrival in California in 1846, Frémont and his men approached Monterey where Mexican General José Castro first welcomed them. After a closer look at the visiting "surveyors," Castro ordered Frémont out. Instead, the Americans dug in on Hawk's Peak, which today is called Fremont Peak. Within three days, the general assembled two-hundred volunteers. That's when Frémont and his five dozen men slipped away, causing Joe Walker, mountain man and parttime guide for the party, to later say, "Frémont morally and physically was the most complete coward I ever knew."

Late in 1846 Frémont led his force and Bear Flag Revolt settlers south on El Camino Real. The Mexicans left Santa Barbara undefended, so he decided his men — nearly five-hundred in all by now — should take a shortcut on an Indian trail over San Marcos Pass, instead of the well-traveled Refugio Pass, and storm the town. E. C. Kemble, a newspaperman with the contingent, wrote in his journal: "Frémont's theory was so absurd that it dropped below criticism at our campfires . . . The foe's well-mounted spies knew all about our movements." The shortcut became a death trap for one-hundred and fifty horses and mules as a heavy storm turned dirt into mud and precipices into slides. Packs, weapons, supplies and cannon littered the trail. Miraculously, no men died.

During the war, Frémont came to San Diego aboard the *Cyane*

"Motley crew" is how Captain Samuel F. du Pont described Frémont's 160-man force after the Cyane's *voyage from Monterey to San Diego. This is one of William Meyers' water colors painted during three years of sea duty.*

with one-hundred and sixty men. They discovered the Mexican commander Andrés Pico and his forces had escaped. The date was July 29, 1846. Don Juan Bandini led the welcoming committee. He believed San Diego had languished because of Mexico's neglect and welcomed the Americans' promise of improved conditions. His daughters sewed old flannels and muslims together for the first American flag flown above the city of some six-hundred people. After a nine-day stay Frémont led his men toward Pueblo de los Angeles astride one of the don's finest sorrels just as Mexican forces began dispanding. Pico surrendered to him January 13, 1847.

Fremont's often unpredictable acts flawed what otherwise stands as a remarkable career. In five expeditions between 1842 and 1853, he explored more territory than Lewis and Clark. His maps, his glowing accounts of the West's potential, his adventures with mountain men and Indians—all made him stand out " . . . as a man who combined all the traits of the Founding Fathers," said his biographer Ferol Egan.

According to historian Josiah Royce, the "faithful knight and hero . . . possessed all the qualities of genius except ability." His main influence on California was to "alienate its people," Royce said.

His post-war defiance of General Stephen W. Kearny's orders finally led to a court martial conviction, but this hardly tarnished the Pathfinder's image in an era when individual initiative earned kudos. Frémont resigned from the Army. A gold strike on his Mother Lode land made the him a millionaire, but the failure of his plan for a second transcontinental railroad all but wiped him out financially.

Fremont was elected one of the first two U. S. senators from California, and the newly formed Republican party chose him as its first presidential candidate. He lost the 1856 election bid mainly because of his anti-slavery stand.

From then until his death in 1890, life held few satisfying vistas for the Pathfinder. Writings by his wife Jessie helped the pair subsist. As Walton Bean and James Rawls said in *California: An Interpretive History*, she once told one of his aides, "Oh, if my husband had only been more positive! But he never did assert himself enough. That was his great fault."

Perhaps. But less impetuosity also might have helped.

Ida Bailey:
Unabashed advertiser

San Diego's reigning madam at the turn of the Twentieth Century wasn't shy about promoting the services of her employees. When a particularly pleasant Sunday rolled around she hired a barouche—a convertible, in today's idiom—from the Diamond Carriage Company. From its shop on Broadway near Second Street the carriage headed to Canary Cottage on Fourth between Market and Island, the most respectable of the hundred or so brothels amidst the Stingaree District. Three employees, dressed in their finest, climbed aboard with her for a sightseeing tour among the city's better residential areas.

Of course, *they* were the sight to behold in what old-timers later realized was San Diego's prototype of mobile outdoor advertising. Occasionally, the carriage stopped along the way so the ladies could hand out a business card or two.

Ida Bailey arrived in the city during the mid-Eighties about the same time local ordinances barred minors from saloons and made solicitation a misdemeanor in various Southern California communities. The California legislature as early as 1855 passed laws against keeping or living in a house of ill fame. The law, however, rarely was enforced because prostitutes already had become an established albeit a peripheral part of society in the West. Women

Ida Bailey and her Canary Cottage consorts shocked society matrons with Sunday carriage rides. She's portrayed here by Nancy Titus at the Horton Grand Hotel.

Stingaree District remnants in 1924 included these 3rd and J street buildings where three and four decades earlier opium dens, saloons, gambling halls and red light houses proliferated.

stood little chance of entering legitimate professions except teaching and nursing. Indeed, in the West, a single, unattached and unemployed woman was automatically pegged as a harlot since so few career possibilities existed.

Moral reforms in 1905 sent prostitutes to a police-protected underground. Madam Bailey's payola insured advance warnings of the sporadic raids, except for one embarrassing time at Canary Cottage when the message didn't arrive. The mayor and two city councilmen reportedly were discovered visiting some constituents but successfully kept the news out of the papers.

Delivery boys pedalled their bikes in from Marston's department store with the latest hats and purses; the respectable sections of commerce being off limits to scarlet women, as prostitutes were sometimes called.

Gamblers and opium den operators shared the Stingaree District shanty town with the ladies of the night. The real estate boom of the mid-Eighties and the frequent arrival of adventure-seeking seamen helped swell the number of houses to about one-hundred and twenty. These included the cribs, the miniscule, windowless rooms a girl rented for fourteen dollars a week plus a percentage for the pimp who also worked as a bouncer. Cribs represented the bottom rung of the prostitute's ladder, the final spot when looks and pride had gone and tricks were sought for fifty cents.

At last in 1912, reformers forced the police to act. Practically the entire force participated in a November 10 raid. A newspaper headline declared: "138 Women Are Arrested in Stingaree Raid" and the subheading said: "136 Promise to Leave City; Two Agree to Reform." The judge suspended each woman's fine of one-hundred dollars providing she would leave San Diego. At the depot many of those heading for Los Angeles reportedly asked for round trip tickets.

When the flapper era arrived, Ida Bailey was seen for a time shuffling into the Second Street station, across from the present day Horton Plaza, visiting the only friends left, the policemen she'd helped support in bygone days.

Ed Fletcher:
A hustler who became senator

Ed Fletcher flubbed his first job in San Diego. A plumbing supply firm hired the sixteen-year-old lad a few days after he arrived from Boston in 1888 with six dollars in his pocket. On the second day, he gave his boss cause for concern. Ed broke eighteen lamp chimneys.

"Friday I put a two-inch brass water faucet high on the shelf, and not too secure," he recalled in his *Memoirs*. "Mr. Johnson (a co-owner) came along and happened to be beneath when a jar of the rack forced the water faucet to fall and hit him squarely on the head. We carried him out unconscious and bleeding. That Saturday night I was fired and sobbed most of the way home."

Armed with the resiliency of youth and a habit of hustling, the handsome, six-foot, three-inch newcomer called on a produce firm operated by M. C. Nason and O. C. Smith. He caught them as Smith lamented the ill-timed purchase of two hundred boxes of apples by Nason.

During a lull in their heated exchange, Ed told why he'd come. "No," one of them snapped, "we don't need any help." This didn't squelch Ed. In Boston, starting at the age of eight, he'd sold newspapers, then peddled fruit door-to-door. At twelve he worked full time in a store's shipping department.

He returned to the produce store and found them still bickering.

"I will sell those apples if you have a horse and wagon I can use," he said with a confidence that persuaded the pair to take a chance. Off he went, visiting grocery stores, restaurants, then the residential areas, working from daybreak until dark. Before a brown spot could surface on his product, he'd sold almost the whole wagon load. Nason and Smith decided they could use some help after all and hired young Fletcher.

All went well during the next seven years except one thing: his pay reached ninety dollars a month — and stayed there. His outside sales experience, however, would later prove a bonanza. He learned the back country's arroyas and mesas and the coastline's inlets and cliffsides. He lugged his bicycle onto the train, then peddled the bike, rain or shine, around towns between stations, selling produce. Once a herd of cattle almost used him as a springboard. Between Vista and San Marcos, over "the worst adobe in California," he toted the bike on his back when the rain turned the roads into goop. By the time he quit and opened his own store in 1895, Fletcher probably knew more about the territory than anyone else in town.

Within a year he paid off the $1,500 he had borrowed to start the business, married his childhood sweetheart Mary and was well on his way to becoming the largest citrus fruit shipper in the county. He also sold eggs, chicks, butter and produce. He met and became friends with people like A. P. Giannini, a young man who would later become head of the Bank of America.

Fletcher's ambition and his love of the region led him out of retailing and into real estate developments. The South Coast Land Company hired him as manager, a fancy title for rights-of-way acquisition work in Pacific Electric Railway's unsuccessful effort to link San Diego and Los Angeles. He also obtained rights for the hydroelectric powerhouse sites along the San Luis Rey River.

Next, the Santa Fe Railroad Company's land department put him on the payroll. As a promoter of the Del Mar and Rancho Santa Fe suburban enclaves, Fletcher tapped his idea tank, creating schemes that attracted home buyers. And buy they did, especially

From the time of he started work at the age of eight, Ed Fletcher began excelling at sales and promotion, but he scored a knockout on his earliest San Diego boss. Fletcher, left, posed on the Mountain Springs Grade with Fred W. Jackson in 1912.

after plans for the the Lake Hodges and Lake Henshaw dams evolved. Built under his supervision, they eased water supply worry, which has long been the San Diego area's chief concern. He also promoted the Mount Helix, Fletcher Hills and Grossmont developments and had a hand in encouraging the Cuyamaca Water Company's growth.

It wasn't all smooth sailing. He put up $25,000 and James A. Murray $125,000 for the Cuyamaca project and Fletcher ended up with a fifteen-year headache because of water leaks and other problems. Out of desperation he tried a rubber-like roofing compound inside a leaky flume line. The stuff worked, saving a $1.4 million line replacement expense. When John D. Spreckels started selling water below cost this caused a rift between the two, but they finally reached a polite if not friendly relationship.

Friends talked Fletcher into running for California's Senate when he was sixty-one. He served a dozen years, battling for highways in the county and the formation of the San Diego County Water Authority. His efforts also led to the establishment of the first Race Relations Commission in the country.

Born in Littleton, Massachusetts, on December 31, 1872, Fletcher, after his mother's death in 1877, was sent to live with his father's cousin. The boy milked eleven cows each day, dug holes and covered up rocks and performed the other mindless farm chores of that day. Life became so bleak he deserted the farm at the age of ten and invited himself to stay with his favorite Sunday school teacher, who lived with her parents.

Fletcher died in 1955 after a life of enthusiastic hustle. Department store owner and philanthropist George W. Marston called him "the prince of promoters." Fletcher's *Memoirs* provide a fascinating glimpse of the man and his times, adding another reason why he will long be remembered.

Alfred H. Isham:
Grandfather of the mineral waters

"**Y**ou scoundrel! You dastardly cad! Get off these premises or I'll throw you off."

Words like these must have exploded from Alfred Huntington Isham when he discovered the man named Sanford had returned. What gall. Such greed.

Isham had learned in 1887 that water from the Jamacha Ranch spring at the base of Mount Miguel contained minerals. He began to bottle and sell it. According to the advertisements he wrote, the water provided unique benefits. Isham's marketing talents, his trips back East paid off. Sales of "Nuvida (New Life) Water" zoomed.

But now Sanford, for the second time, had persuaded Isham's employee to place "Sanford's Elixer" labels on the bottles in a takeover attempt as bold as a Boetsky.

Caught again in the act, Sanford, a San Francisco land developer, went bonkers. He pulled out a pistol and fired. The bullet missed Isham and grazed the person of one Charles Fitzfallen. Sanford fled and Fitzfallen quickly recovered, no doubt because of the healthy water.

Isham's employee, a Mrs. Chittenden, revealed Sanford's ploy. The wily interloper had softened her with her favorite chocolates, persuaded her he owned the property and that Isham's leasing arrangement didn't, ah, hold water.

Renewed marketing efforts and a change in the name to "Isham's California Water of Life" helped increase the product's popularity in many sections of the United States. It was a forerunner of Perrier by almost a century. Part of the appeal stemmed from Isham's ads.

The spring water " . . . possesses a unique power, probably electrolytic, to actually retard old age, grow hair on bald heads, expel morbid products and ineffective organisms, and completely rebuild the tissue of the human body."

This almost seems understated when compared with other ads of that era. The results proved profitable, but big profits proved the undoing of Isham. The former window-sash weight salesman began spending his time and money on frivolous pasttimes. Before long his riches vaporized.

According to Herbert Lockwood in *The Skeleton's Closet,* the opportunity for a last minute recovery arose when J. Claudine Potts, the firm's representative in Philadelphia, picked up a midwinter order for three carloads of bottled water. Potts persuaded a glass company to ship $15,000 worth of bottles on credit.

At the Mount Miguel spring site a contrite Isham injected the water and arranged for the return shipment. No one knows if Isham had been drinking something other than his water or if the railroad goofed, but the three carloads of bottled water traveled by way of Montana instead of the intended New Orleans route. When the water froze, the bottles cracked, broke or exploded. Perhaps that's what shattered the health of Alfred Huntington Isham. He died broke in 1910 from an undisclosed cause.

The Incredible

Bum:

A town dog with panache

On the day that a new dog catcher apprehended Bum, the fellow made a mistake by dragging the dog past a group of downtown rowdies. Several of them pounced on the public servant cuffing him about the ears while shouting rude remarks about the ancestry of anyone so callous as to abduct the town's mascot. Meanwhile, the others removed the dog's wire restrainer.

News of the incident spread quickly through San Diego. Residents welcomed this latest evidence that people from all walks of life loved and respected Bum, part St. Bernard, part spaniel and part charmer. The dog had arrived in the city late in 1886. He had stowed away, it was said, on a steamer from San Francisco.

In his new surroundings, Bum adopted a fisherman, one Ah Wo Sue. But in the tradition of true town dogs, Bum declined a permanent one-family tie, and soon claimed all of the 20,000 or so residents as his own. Some, though, were so busy buying and selling real estate that year they paid scant attention to anything without wooden lot line stakes and strings around it.

Bum included the Santa Fe Railroad yard as part of his turf. A tough bulldog contested the claim. He and Bum battled it out and ended up in the path of an oncoming engine. The bulldog died and

Where Bum parked people gathered. That's why newsboys welcomed his visits, they sold more papers. His aristocratic bearing impressed chefs, who gave him scraps.

Bum lost his right forepaw and a piece of his tail. He limped back temporarily to Ah Wo Sue who nursed the wounds. Despite the disability, Bum one day picked up a small dog off a street railway track, carrying it to safety moments before a trolley zoomed by.

His aristocratic mien persuaded butchers and restaurant chefs that a sample was his due, not a donation. In a kingly fashion, he would choose the center of a sidewalk to hold court, and the subjects flowed cheerfully around and some stopped to pay homage. Newsboys appreciated the dog because he invariably attracted fans, many of whom bought a paper.

One might have guessed his middle name was Spreckels, the way he freeloaded on the train. A few conductors, unaware of his status, led him back to the baggage car, but usually he traveled first class. The San Diego telegrapher alerted telegraphers along the line, so on a jaunt to, say, Los Angeles, Bum received a cordial welcome, even an occasional tour.

Parades and fires kept him in shape. He headed their way whenever the music from a band or the clanging sounded. He also helped welcome President Benjamin Harrison on his visit in April 1891 and frequently stood at attention when the bugle sounded at the military parade grounds.

That same year the city council heard a plea that Bum deserved a dog tag good for life, an idea based "on the grounds that he did more to advertise the city and county than most of the newspapers."

This suggestion came from James E. "Captain" Friend, a roving stringer for the *San Diego Union* who arrived in town about the same time as Bum. In those days the city council could and did act speedily on pressing matters. So Bum got tagged for life. In fact, dog licenses that year bore his likeness.

This about coincided with Bum's greatest challenge — or opportunity, depending on one's personal point of view. Some men either coaxed or forced hard liquor down the dog's throat. He developed a craving for the stuff. Before long, his behavior matched his name. Not until the kindly, unjudgmental Ah Wo Sue initiated a drying out program did Bum regain his standing in the community.

This alleged bout with booze was just so much balderdash, according to some observers of the San Diego scene then. They maintain Bum at times acted, well, like most dogs, but he never succumbed to demon rum.

At the age of twelve — about sixty-five on the human scale of years — and crippled with rheumatism, he was taken to the county hospital where he died in 1898. Captain Friend, the man who chronicled many of Bum's adventures, perhaps even embellished a few, died a few months later.

Recalling those times and the city's temperament, Mrs. Martha Brix a few years later sent a letter to the editor: "Bum is more than a memory; he is a symbol of San Diego. He stands for much that we need today — loyalty, faithfulness and devotion."

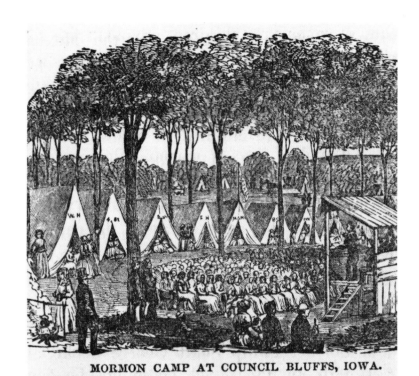

MORMON CAMP AT COUNCIL BLUFFS, IOWA.

At Brigham Young's direction, 536 Mormons enlisted in the battalion and began a trek of about 2,200 miles; 365 men and four women made it into San Diego.

The Mormon Battalion:
When the Saints came marching in

"**H**istory may be searched in vain for an equal march of infantry," said Lt. Colonel P. St. George Cooke after the Mormon Battallion in 1847 completed a trek of some 2,200 miles to San Diego. His tribute continued:

"Half of it has been through a wilderness where nothing but savages and wild beasts are found, or deserts, where, for want of water, there is no living creature . . . We have dug wells, which the future traveler will enjoy . . . With crowbar and pick and ax in hand, we have worked our way over mountains, which seemed to defy aught save the wild goat, and hewed a passage through a chasm of living rock more narrow than our wagons . . . Thus, marching half-naked, and half fed, and living upon wild animals, we have discovered and made a road of great value to our country."

A total of five-hundred and thirty-six Latter-day Saints men had enlisted in the battalion at Council Bluffs, Iowa, in mid-July the year before. The sign-up represented a shrewd move on the part of their leader, Brigham Young. President James K. Polk, in looking ahead for a United States in a mood of expansionist discovery, envisioned a string of forts across the plains into the Far West. The forts would provide havens for the coming wave of settlers.

Polk's plan gave Brigham Young two ways by which his people could benefit: 1) Because of persecution being inflicted on the Mormons, he had already decided they should head West. Here was the chance to work their way across the country, complete with foodstuffs and tools, plus safeguards against Indians and the elements. 2) The public surely would view his Saints with more respect and understanding once they completed the fort-building project.

But the United States, provoked by an attack, declared war on Mexico before Brigham Young's emissary reached Washington, D. C. with the proposal. Polk asked Brigham Young if his men would serve in a special battalion, helping the virtually non-existent United States military force in California. The Mormon leader said yes. He calculated that the soldiers' pay and an advance on expenses could help sustain the Saints who were fleeing from their Nauvoo, Illinois, settlement toward the Great Basin in Utah.

So the volunteers, many of them dubious about leaving their families, marched from Council Bluffs to Fort Leavenworth, Kansas. Thirty-six wives went along as laundresses. Fifty children also came.

They began their epic journey July 20, 1846 under the command of Captain James Allen of the First Dragoons. He died on the trail and was succeeded by Lt. Colonel Cooke. The objective: reach the battle area with as many able bodied men and as much military supplies as possible.

Deserts, rivers, mountains, the dreaded cholera—all took a toll. From Fort Mann, Kansas, the children and thirty-two wives were escorted to Pueblo, Colorado, for the winter. One-hundred and forty-eight men headed east from Sante Fe to Pueblo as part of a Sick Detachment. Seven men died along the way. Several were reassigned. John Allen of Company E was drummed out for unspecified misconduct.

The caravan ventured into unexplored territory in southwestern New Mexico across the Continental Divide near Guadalupe Pass. At one stage of the journey, the party swung below the United States-Mexico border until Scott called for a shift in direction, a decision some of the Saints believed resulted from God's guiding hand.

According to Norma B. Ricketts in *Mormons and the Discovery of Gold*, the battalion members straggled into California on bleeding bare feet, ravenous, their clothes in tatters. Their weary pack animals pulled what remained of the wagons. A year earlier,

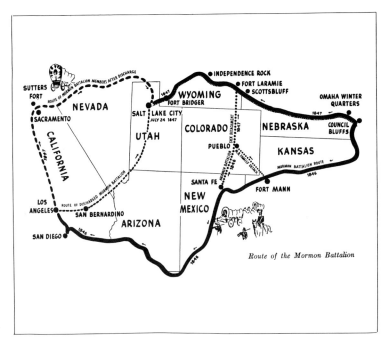

Most of the wives and and all of the children headed for Pueblo from Ft. Mann and 148 sick men detoured from Santa Fe for the winter camp in Colorado. (Map adapted from Mormons and the Discovery of Gold *with permission of Norma B. Ricketts.)*

General Stephen W. Kearny and his men were forced to abandon their wagons along the same general trail because of the rugged terrain. When the general learned that the Mormons had arrived, he sent word that the war with Mexico was over, at least in California, and ordered them to head for San Diego. Three-hundred and sixty-five men and four wives made camp near the abandoned mission where a few Indians peered at these new-comers who looked as impoverished as they did.

After a few days, Lt. Colonel Scott sent a small group to Mission San Luis Rey; four other companies headed to Los Angeles. The men in the remaining San Diego company, with no soldiering required and true to their traditions of industry and thrift, began tackling chores in the tacky town of San Diego.

"I think I whitewashed all of San Diego," said Henry G. Boyle in

The relief of water and rest by a river is dramatazed in this G.M. Ottinger painting of the battalion. (Church of Jesus Christ of Latter-day Saints photo.)

his journal. "We did their blacksmithing, put up a bakery, made and repaired carts and, in time, did all we could to benefit ourselves as well as the citizens. We never had any trouble with Californians or Indians, nor they with us."

No wonder amity prevailed. In San Diego, soldiers were synonymous with trouble. They had stolen, caroused and abused others. These Mormons abstained, behaved courteously and acted like, well, Saints. They built the town's first brick house across from the Plaza, installed fifteen or twenty wells, some of them with log pumps, which the locals had not seen before. No wonder the townspeople wanted these paragons to reenlist when their departure time came.

The Mormon company marched up to Los Angeles. Their mustering out pay helped buy the fort and trappers' site that today is Ogden, Utah. San Diegans found cause for rejoicing when eighty-five of the Saints signed on for a six-month hitch and returned.

Jesse Hunter's wife Lydia gave birth to a son, but as so often happened on the frontier, she died in child birth. Diego, as the infant was named, was the first child born in San Diego whose parents were both Americans.

The Mormon Battalion blazed a trail for later settlers as well as for a transcontinental railroad line and a highway which would eventually be built. The battalion's loyalty, performance and perserverance earned the respect of the San Diegans, then the dragoons and ultimately the public at large — just as Brigham Young had hoped they would.

Indian home like this one on Warner's ranch probably served as shelter for William Marshall and his wife. He ran Warner's trading store and bar.

William Marshall and Antonio Garra:
Patsy and principal
of the '51 revolt

A San Diego County census in 1847 showed 1,550 wild Indians, 483 converted Indians, 248 white people, three blacks and three Hawaiians, or Sandwich Island natives, as they were known. These ratios remained much the same by the time Agoston Haraszthy became the county's first sheriff four years later. His job included collecting taxes and, noting that some Indians possessed livestock, he sought payment from them as he made his rounds. He included them among his constituency even though it was illegal for them to vote.

Antonio Garra, chief of the Cupeños tribe near the Warner's Ranch, viewed things a bit differently than Haraszthy. Educated at the San Luis Rey Mission, Garra had grown up in a time when nearly two-thirds of his people died of diseases introduced by the white man. They had taken the Indians' land with the only payment as often as not a rifle bullet for anyone bold enough to protest. Some of the latecomers employed them as serfs or abused them like slaves.

So Chief Garra reached a decison. He called for a revolt. Including tribes in Baja California, the Central Valley and the Colorado River region, he could count on outnumbering the enemy by about ten to one, if he could persuade the Indians they should set aside their differences and unite in an uprising.

Meanwhile, **William Marshall,** operator of a combination store, saloon and pawn shop at Warner's Hot Springs, had married the daughter of another chief, Jose Nocar. Marshall's talent for attracting trouble had led him to jump ship in 1845 while the whaler *Hopewell* was anchored in San Diego Bay. His non-involvement stance in the war with Mexico caused his arrest the following year for disloyalty. In 1847 he won an acquittal when John J. Warner charged him with stealing.

By November, 1851 word circulated that the Indians might go on the warpath. Garra rode with the Yumas during a sheep stealing foray in which at least two herdsmen died. On the day scheduled for the first major assault, however, he announced that illness prevented him from taking part. So some Cahuillas warriors joined with the Cupeños and girded for battle without him.

According to Marshall's version, the Indians told him war had been declared. His choice: join them or die. His sidekick Juan Verdugo received the same ultimatum. They enlisted. On November 22 one Indian party attacked Warner's ranch. Forewarned, Warner had sent his family and servants to San Diego and, with gun blazing, he escaped. Four men at the Hot Springs were not so fortunate. They were murdered the night before.

In San Diego unmarried men joined the "Fitzgerald Volunteers," named for the Army major who led them. They failed in the first attempt to avenge the Hot Springs murders, but they did return with Marshall, his father-in-law and Verdugo. "The Indians held us prisoner," said Marshall.

In the court martial that followed, Marshall's own mother-in-law testified he was guilty of robbery and murder, as charged. The court decided, no, he was guilty of high treason. Not that it made much difference. Still protesting his innocence, the Providence, Rhode Island, native was hanged December 13 along with Verdugo, who admitted his guilt.

Historian Lelan E. Bibb has noted that a California law on the books then stated, "In no case shall a white man be convicted of any

One reason William Marshall may have jumped ship from the whaler Hopewell *could have been the hard work and the olefactory impact suggested by this picture.*

offense upon the testimony of an Indian," but the tribunal either ignored or knew nothing of the statute.

Bibb believes the rapid frontier justice stemmed from a need for a scapegoat. Americans disliked facing the evidence that the Indians, so long regarded as ignorant and ineffectual, could plan and nearly succeed with an uprising. Marshall, after all, lived with them and even married one. This was tantamount to guilt in the eyes of his captors.

Thirty years afterward, Marshall was mistakenly implicated in in the 1846 Pauma Massacre. Which shows he could even attract trouble dead.

Antonio Garra, seeking support from the Cahuillas, was instead turned over by their chief to the volunteer army. Garra was found guilty and sentenced to die before a firing squad. "The officials made this charge hold because of the evidence that Garra had not paid taxes to San Diego County," according to Max Miller in *Harbor of the Sun*.

Garra's guards led him beside an open grave. There Padre Juan Holbein told him to request the pardon of the large crowd waiting for the firing squad's volley. Garra refused. The priest insisted. At last the chief looked up, smiled and said, "Gentlemen, I ask your pardon for all my offenses, and expect yours in return."

Gleason's Pictorial Drawing Room Companion *said Indian chiefs like this lost their occupation because of the influx of the white man and "must submit to the force of circumstances."*

Josie and Wyatt Earp:
Harmony of a sort in San Diego

There is reason to suspect Josie and Wyatt Earp experienced more than an average number of spats during their years together. In their fifth year, soon after moving to San Diego in 1885, she conceived a technique that restored harmony.

During flare-ups "I fell back . . . on my handiest weapon, words," she recalled in *I Married Wyatt Earp*. "If what I said did not rile my husband too much, he simply grinned and took it. But when I got him mad he would fill and light his pipe, put on his hat and walk out. Any wife who has had this happen knows that it is the most exasperating thing a husband can do to her. Tears do no good with no one to see them."

One day after his exit ritual, she wrote down what she'd intended to tell him. "By then I was beginning to think it was funny and must have conveyed that in my note," she said. She visited a friend next door until he returned, then walked in.

"There was Wyatt, hands in his pockets, reading my note, a broad grin on his face. We looked at each other and laughed." Earp thereafter called the notes her "love letters" and told friends they always gave her the last word.

The technique helps explain how the couple made their common-law marriage work despite his being a "skirt chaser," as womanizers were once known, and despite the suspicion that Josie

Only 24 when she and Wyatt arrived in San Diego, Josie Earp liked the excitement at the track after he won a horse in a poker game and developed a stable of trotters.

Quick and graceful, Wyatt Earp earned spare cash as a prize fight referee during a dozen years in San Diego. He also operated three downtown gambling halls.

engaged in an occasional peccadillo. Or so says Glenn G. Boyer, who spent more than thirty years researching the life of Wyatt Earp and edited the two manuscripts that comprise Josie's book of recollections.

Josephine Sarah Marcus Earp admitted, "I sometimes flew off the handle over little things." A friend of her husband told him that the main reason he never married was the fear of a union with a shrew like Josie. Her charm, however, when she chose to exhibit it, her beauty and zest for life more than offset her peevishness, at least in her husband's eyes.

As in all their travels, the dream of hitting paydirt lured them to San Diego. Wyatt had heard about a real estate boom and decided they could capitalize on it. He soon established three gambling halls in the downtown area. Then he won a trotting horse in a poker game, and added several more to his string. He and Josie barnstormed around the state's race tracks, their fortunes fluctuating on the horses' speed, the gambling revenues and San Diego's real estate ups and downs.

Wyatt and Josie had moved about in Colorado, Idaho and Texas before reaching San Diego. She was twenty-four and he was thirty-seven when they arrived. Handsome, muscular and well groomed, Wyatt Earp by this time was gaining folk hero status because of the Tombstone, Arizona, shootout in 1881 with the Clanton gang near the O. K. Corral. He possessed "a strange power over men," said his friend Bat Masterson, who had teamed with him during Earp's day as a Dodge City marshall.

Regarded as a good ally in a brawl, Earp occasionally refereed prizefights while living in San Diego. When the Fitzsimmons-Sharkey match rolled around, he bet a bundle on the heavily favored Fitzsimmons. The promoters asked him to referee the San Francisco match. He finally agreed at the eleventh hour, and called off as many of his bets as possible. Fitzsimmons fouled Sharkey, so Earp awarded the decision to the underdog. Fitzsimmons' backers vilified Earp, claiming he imagined the low blow and profited from the call. Doctors who examined Sharkey supported Earp, but the hullaballo buttressed Earp's wish to someday escape notoriety and pressures of city life. He longed for the desert, especially an area where gold or silver gleamed, or for the range country where a fellow could raise a few head of cattle.

His horse racing sideline led to a friendship with Elias Jackson Baldwin who owned the Santa Anita Ranch near Los Angeles and the Baldwin Hotel in San Francisco. Baldwin had acquired a fortune trading his Comstock Lode mining stock as it peaked, thus earning the nickname "Lucky." Baldwin's weakness for pretty young women proved risky: two of them nicked him on separate occasions with pistol bullets after deciding he'd trifled with their affections.

"He had many friends, who seemed to care sincerely for him," Josie said. "He was an entertaining companion, and because of mutual interest, Wyatt and I saw a lot of him."

Josie had cut loose from her San Francisco home at the age of eighteen with an *H. M. S. Pinafore* troupe and met Wyatt soon after breaking her engagement to lawman Johnny Behan. Wyatt, a Monmouth, Illinois, native, grew up on a farm near Pella, Iowa. His first wife died in childbirth along with their infant. Following this, a horse stealing count against a Wyatt S. Earp turned up at Ft. Smith Arkansas. The culprit skipped bail. Earp and his second wife, Celia Ann Blaylock, were married or living together before their arrival in Tombstone in 1879. They apparently had separated before Josie met him there.

Josie and Wyatt Earp found a cottage in Vidal, California, not far from Parker, Arizona, where they spent their winters during their last twenty-five years together.

Earp died on January 13, 1929 at the age of eighty-one. Josie lived to the age of eighty-three. They both had fond memories of San Diego. "Wyatt and I had some of our most wonderful times together there," she said.

Quotations by permission from I Married Wyatt Earp: The Recollections of Josephine Sarah Marcus Earp, *edited by Glenn G. Boyer, Tucson: University of Arizona Press, copyright 1976.*

In a report to his superiors, Portolá said that if the Russians wanted Alta California, let them have it. It might teach them to mend their expansionist ways.

Gaspar de Portolá:
The doubting captain

A lta California's **first governor** and commandant, Captain Gaspar de Portolá, probably began counting the cost on July 1, 1769, two days after reaching San Diego by land from New Spain. Here's how his summary might have looked:

1. Father Junipero Serra arrived today and amazes all with his recovery from ulcerated foot/leg that almost forced his return by land to Loreta.

2. Thirty-eight men dead of scurvy, many others near death, most of them from *San Carlos*, which took one-hundred and ten days arriving from La Paz. *San Antonio* crew in better shape; only fifty-four days at sea. No sign of *San Jose*; presumed lost at sea because of scurvy decimating crew.

3. Unknown disease taking toll of land expedition men also. Of total land/sea force of 300 men, almost half are dead or missing. This includes land party's Christianized Indians whose rations were discontinued after supplies grew short; some deserted.

4. Local Indians grow bolder. They steal blankets of sick men as death approaches. They leave what little food remains untouched.

5. Supplies nearly gone.

P ortolá **assigned eight men** to sail the *San Antonio* back for supplies and more men. Two weeks after reaching San Diego, he headed north with Padre Juan Crespi, engineer Miguel Costansó and those soldiers, muleteers and Indians still able to walk. Having established San Diego as a way station, at least in name, their next goal was to establish a presidio, or military garrison, in Monterey. Then the British and Russians could see Spain still held firm control of the Pacific Coast.

That at least represented the thinking of José de Galvez, the visitor-general of New Spain. Father Serra's missions would help civilize the area and provide economic stability for natives and future Spanish settlers.

Portolá's party experienced earthquakes, befriended Indians and slogged along spots that later would be known as Santa Barbara, San Luis Obispo and Los Angeles. But when they reached Monterey they didn't recognize it. Sebastián Vizcaíno had described it as "Puerto Monterey," indicating a closed harbor like San Diego's rather than an open bay. The hungry band of men could not see the *San Jose* at anchor, which also indicated they should continue north.

A t the sight of San Francisco Bay, a sickly Portolá remained unimpressed, but Father Crespi wrote in his journal, "It is a very large and fine harbor, such that not only all the navy of our most Catholic Majesty but those of all Europe could take shelter in it."

The men turned back, surviving on the return trip by eating a dozen of their mules. They reached San Diego January 24, 1770. Not one to give up or disregard orders, Portolá headed north again April 17 and this time recognized the features of Monterey, which Vizcaíno had described. Father Serra arrived on the *San Antonio* a week later to establish Alta (Upper) California's headquarters mission.

In their book *California: An Interpretive History*, Walton Bean and James Rawls state that Portolá from the beginning had misgivings about the entire undertaking. Officials in Mexico City at first rejoiced after Portolá's expedition, but his frank report upset them. Portolá said that if the Russians want that territory let them have it; it might make them regret their expansionist ways. Spain could not thwart Russian inroads along the California coast "unless it was proposed to sacrifice thousands of men and huge sums of money," he declared.

Born about 1723 in Balaguer, Catalonia, Portolá went on after his California expeditions to become a lieutenant colonel in the royal Spanish Army. He was appointed governor of Puebla in 1777, then ordered back to Spain seven years later shortly before his death.

An Irish proverb says, "Good luck beats early rising," But if General Stephen Kearny had attacked early, he might have claimed a legitimate victory at San Pasquale.

General Stephen W. Kearny:
The hard-luck commander

The battle of San Pasquale stands out as the major confronta-
tion on California soil during the war between the United
States and Mexico. It also stands out for the invaders as a classic
example of Murphy's Law.* And as luck would have it, another
Irishman, Stephen W. Kearny, shouldered the responsibility for a
devastating "victory."

General Kearny was enroute to California from New Mexico
with three-hundred dragoons — armed cavalrymen. On October 3,
1846, almost five months after the war began, the troops bumped
into Kit Carson, which proved unfortunate because he carried
dispatches from Commodore Robert F. Stockton declaring California "free from Mexican dominion." Los Angeles had fallen without
a shot being fired. This persuaded Kearny. He sent two-hundred
dragoons back to Santa Fe. He also convinced Carson that he
should return to California with Kearny's remaining men.

Carson knew the trail, but erred one-hundred and eighty degrees about the fighting capability of the *Californios*. "They are
cowards," he told Kearny. Thus, when the dragoons reached San
Pasquale, sixty-five miles north, northeast of San Diego, the general decided to attack a force of about eighty men led by Andrés
Pico. The Americans had struggled over 2,000 miles of rugged
terrain. They needed fresh mounts. So, despite the numbing cold

---

The principle that whatever can possibly go wrong will.

Mexico's General Andrés Pico needed proof about the gringo's presence before the San Pasquale battle. Once convinced, he led his troops in an attack that killed 20 percent of Kearny's worn out dragoons, while suffering only a few casualties.

rain, the hunger, the worn out mules and horses, the dragoons prepared for a pre-dawn surprise attack on December 6. Kearny and his officers had discussed strategy the previous day. The general called for a scouting patrol, but Captain Benjamin Moore suggested the whole force should attack at the same time. The enemy surely would hear or spot a patrol, he said. If they did, all chances would be lost of surprising them without their horses. "To dismount them is to whip them," he added. Kearny vetoed Moore.

Just as Moore predicted, Pico's men detected the ten-man reconnaissance group. At first Pico refused to believe the news. Not until his men showed him an Army blanket and a dragoon's jacket dropped by the gringos did he realize a battle approached.

At 3 a.m. the exhausted dragoons, two by two, began their advance along an unfamiliar trail. When they came within striking distance, Kearny gave the order, "Trot." Up front, this was misinterpreted as "Charge!" So the advance rank moved into the battle zone with the rest of the dragoons spread out behind.

Incredibly, they had not recharged their arms. Their damp ammunition failed to fire. The *Californios*, riding like circus performers, wielded their long lances with deadly effect that foggy morning. They attacked, fell back, then ambushed the invaders, who could only use their rifles as clubs. Twenty-two of the dragoons died and sixteen were wounded, including the General.

The battle ended when the dragoons fired one or two rounds from a pair of howitzers, according to some accounts of the battle. Another version says the *Californios* lassooed a cannon with their reatas and in the hulabaloo of hauling it away encouraged a withdrawal.

Kit Carson's horse stumbled in the initial charge. Uninjured in the fall, he and Lieutenant Edward F. Beale and one of the Indian guides went for help. They removed their shoes so they could sneak past three of the enemy's lines, losing their shoes in the process. They split to reduce the risk of capture and walked barefoot nearly thirty miles for help. After it arrived, the bedraggled Americans limped into San Diego December 12, 1846.

Kearny declared the battle of San Pasquale a victory since the enemy departed the scene. Four more victories like that, however, and his whole force would have been annihilated. The Mexican forces scattered and began squabbling. Andrés Pico surrendered to John Charles Frémont, who then tried running the show as California governor, a rank Commodore Stockton conferred. Kearny's orders clearly showed he should be in charge, but Frémont stubbornly refused his commands. Finally General Kearny ordered Frémont's arrest.

In the court martial that followed, Frémont and his father-in-law, the powerful Senator Thomas Hart Benton, pilloried Kearny with misstatements and innuendos. Found guilty of mutiny and insubordination, Frémont resigned from the Army. Ironically, the public judged Kearny guilty of too harsh a reaction based partly on Frémont's lack of a West Point diploma. Yet Kearny himself had not graduated from the academy.

Born on August 30, 1794 in Newark, New Jersey, Stephen Watts Kearny was the eleventh child in a family that that would total fifteen children in all. He enrolled in Kings College, a predecessor to Columbia University, but left for action in the war of 1812. He remained in the Army and displayed ingenuity and dedication as he moved up the ranks to commander of the Army of the West.

Following the armistice with Mexico in 1848, Kearny's luck failed to improve. The Army assigned him civil governor of Vera Cruz, where he contracted yellow fever. He died from it on October 31, 1848, two weeks after the birth of his eleventh child, a boy. His wife Mary named him Stephen Watts Kearny, Jr.

William Rosecrans:
The outmaneuvered general

A one-hundred gun salute found almost all of San Diego's 2,000 or so residents on hand to greet General William S. Rosecrans on his first visit April 14, 1866. The throng showed how commerce and convenience sometimes outweigh conviction; most of the greeters were "copperheads" — southern sympathizers — and the general had served brilliantly throughout most of the Civil War — for the Yankees.

The noisy crowd ignored that fact. They turned out because of the general's big financial stake in the Southern Pacific Railroad. The SP, according to rumors, might extend a railroad line all the way to San Diego. Rosecrans, however, was merely enroute for an update on another investment possibility, the copper mines across the border.

When he returned the next year, the San Diegans saved their cannon balls, even though the visitor's trip this time related to railroading. Rosecrans had been a shrewd if outspoken war strategist and a talented engineer. His marks fell short, though, in the business world's wheeling and dealing. Sharpies arranged to buy his railroad stock at an unpublicized auction after the general failed to pay an assessment on it. The notice, published as required, appeared in a newspaper he normally did not see. The culprits also sent squatters onto his land, but he managed to save the property, according to Richard F. Pourade in *The Glory Years*.

Alonzo Horton met Rosecrans on that second visit. They

Red carpet treatment for General William Rosecrans proved fruitless: his monetary interest in railroads did not help San Diego establish the connection it wanted.

teamed with Ephraim Morse and several other business leaders for some railroad line reconnoitering. The general liked the Jacumba Pass route although the Army Engineers and General W. J. Palmer in separate reports had nixed it previously. Rosecrans persisted and allied himself with another general, John C. Frémont. Frémont had acquired rights and consolidated several companies, hoping to build the nation's second transcontinental rairoad.

Once again Rosecrans departed after a brief stay. He returned a third time in 1869 along with Secretary of State William H. Seward, several congressmen, Frémont's representative, General Morton C. Hunter, and the chief engineer of the Memphis & El Paso Railroad, one of the companies under Frémont's control. San Diego turned out en masse and heard what they longed to know: the Memphis and El Paso planned to start construction soon for the next cross-country line.

The city fathers pledged half a million dollars worth of land and rights in exchange for stock certificates. But the Memphis & El Paso folded the following year. Frémont lost the fortune he had acquired from a lucky Mother Lode gold find. San Diego's railroad-related inferiority complex worsened.

Rosecrans departed for good, but his name remains in prominent view for San Diegans. The Army established Fort Rosecrans Military Reservation on Point Loma in 1899 and today it includes the nation's second largest military cemetery. His name also appears on the signs along the San Diego boulevard and street named for him.

Born in Kingston, Ohio, on September 6, 1819, William Starke Rosecrans quickly was nicknamed "Rosy" after enrolling at West Point where he was described by fellow cadets as gregarious and in high spirits. One cadet noted that he talked "interestingly, daily, fast, his imagination racing." It proved a trait which later created problems, especially when he critiqued his superiors. He majored in engineering and after graduation taught the subject at West Point.

He then resigned, partly because of health, but mainly for added money to support his wife and four children. Rosecrans became a partner with a Cincinnati businessman in a kerosene producing venture. A patented so-called safety lamp exploded and the burns left vivid facial scars. His beard covered the permanent "smirk" caused by the accident. He invented a lamp with a round wick and discovered how to make a colorless, odorless kerosene, but as the business began showing a profit, the Civil War began.

As an aide-de-camp in the Ohio Volunteers, he served under G. B. McLellan and began leading a series of crucial victories over the Confederates. These led to his appointment to brigadier general. His men liked Rosy; he invariably showed up in the front lines during battles. His candid comments about the mistakes and ineptitude of superior officers, combined with a crushing defeat in the Battle of Chickamauga in 1863, caused a reassignment to the Department of Missouri, comparable to a Soviet officer's banishment to Siberia. He resigned early in 1867.

After his San Diego excursions, Rosecrans returned to the Los Angeles area where voters elected him a Congressional representative for two terms. He served as the minister to Mexico from 1868 to 1869 and United States Treasury register. His final years were spent in Redondo.

Kate Sessions:
San Diego's exterior decorator

A friend asked Kate Sessions for help. "After all, your advertising slogan says 'Plants, trees, shrubs and *advice.*' What sort of tree should we plant in that sandy area in front of the North Mission Clubhouse?"

"Plant a deodora," Kate said.

It took hold beautifully. Then one day she drove by and spied the groundskeeper cutting off the last of its lower limbs. It seems when the wind blew, the branches and leaves disrupted the pattern he painstakingly raked in the sand each day. Kate dashed from the car and confronted the man.

"Look at me," she bellowed as she hoisted her lengthy skirt above her knees, revealing lumpy black stockings protruding over a pair of men's shoes. "Do I look pretty with my dress like this? That's the way you made that tree look."

And judging from the recollections of people who worked with her or for her, she probably added a few expletives as well, underscoring her displeasure.

Katherine Olivia Sessions felt strongly about plants. They were the love of her life. And for most of her eighty-three years, she studied, talked about, grew and promoted little else. "The Mother of Balboa Park" as she became known, started the love affair about the time her parents moved from San Francisco to Oakland. She was six.

"I want to hoe the weeds," she told her uncle. When he came to inspect, she'd demolished his cabbages. In a trouble-free and enjoyable childhood she collected, dried and pressed plants, even neatly noted where she found them. She was attractive and popular. A few problems surfaced, however, according to a diary she began in 1876 at the age of nineteen. Headaches, eye strain and "feeling miserable" entries suggested a change of pace might help. Her biographer Elizabeth MacPhail suggests this as one theory to account for her sudden decision to join friends of the family on a trip to Hawaii.

During the two-month visit Sessions fell for the poinsettias and the palm trees, both of which became her specialties later.

After a stint of teaching in Oakland, she moved to San Diego to become a principal and teacher at the Russ School, named for a generous lumber yard owner. She left when her operating funds dried up. The Solon Blaisdelles, who knew about her botanical and agricultural studies at the University of California in Berkeley, invited her to join them as a partner for a new nursery and flower shop. They provided seed money, she supplied the know-how. Soon brisk sales enabled them to build a glass hot house on Coronado, but the partners decided to split nonetheless. "The Blaisdelles were old people and conservative," she later told a friend. "I was young and full of ambition. The partnership did not last very long, but we divided the assets and I had my start."

S he hustled. Seven days a week her eight to six routine included a ferry boat ride from the new flower shop to Coronado and back. In 1892 she obtained the city council's approval to lease thirty acres of what was then called City Park and agreed to annually plant one-hundred trees in the park and donate three-hundred more for use elsewhere in exchange for rent-free use of the land. To thwart any note of impropriety they named her San Diego gardener. Thus began a decade of importing exotic plants and seeds, infusing workers with her fervor, enlisting help from community leaders.

As the park blossomed and her nursery business flowered, her appearance became rather seedy. She cared little about how she looked or what she said. She began wearing men's boots. She tromped about the 1,400-acre park and everyplace she dug her heel into the turf a plant soon followed. One of her mottos: A fifty cent tree should be planted in a five dollar hole, meaning lots of room for

Kate Sessions, the Mother of Balboa Park, worked seven days a week.

roots to take hold. Pockets sewn onto her generous skirts provided room for shears, gloves and miscellany.

In her two-cylinder Maxwell she became one of San Diego's first woman drivers. Once she left the engine on and came back to find the car slowly circling in the street. She hopped on the running board, not quite sure how to stop it, all the time hollering "Whoa!

Whoa!" Soon afterwards she hired a driver.

When the Park Improvement Committee she'd encouraged hired New York landscaping architect, Samuel Parsons Jr., who created New York City's Central Park, she worked closely with him, offering ideas on unusual specimens and continuing with her plantings. She agreed with his view that Balboa Park was "unequaled in its natural beauty and potentiality." They won a skirmish with people who believed lakes and dams in the canyon would enhance the park, but lost the battle of keeping simple the Panama-California Exposition of 1915. As it turned out, though, the ornate Spanish Mediterranean buildings caught the public's fancy. Nearly 3.7 million people attended.

Sessions moved her business twice, shying away from commercial and residential encroachments. At Mission Hills, she let John D. Spreckels know she'd appreciate having his electric trolleys extend to her street.

"Fair enough," he evidently told her. "I'll do it if you can get Lewis and Washington streets widened."

She and her assistant promptly began house-to-house calls with petitions. After enough signatures were collected she presented the documents to the city council, which authorized the widening.

Along with the city's adulation came many honors. The one most cherished was winning the Frank N. Meyer medal from the American Genetic Association, which annually recognized a horticulturist for the introduction of outstanding flowers and plants. This came when she was eighty-one. It was the fifteenth presentation of the medal and she was the first woman to receive it.

Her father joined her firm after the death of his wife, then her brother Frank also joined. The father had farmed and his talk was speckled with cuss words. His daughter Kate incorporated most of them, although she tried to convince others she relied on obscure Latin plant terminology to motivate employees. With the passing years she became quite deaf and as so often happens she compensated for it by talking louder. Toward the end some callow San Diegans regarded her as a comical character. But as Elizabeth MacPhail points out, "She was one of the state's first environmentalists and conservationists long before the terms became popular . . . "

One of Balboa Park's most unusual features is its Palm Canyon,

Trees and plants provide living reminders of creative landscaping ideas.

More than 50 types of Kate Sessions' favorite tree grow in Palm Canyon.

which includes more than fifty species of palms, many of them ones she'd planted following a trip to Baja California with some horticulturists. She returned with numerous seeds and small plants.

Her trees and shrubs and flowers spruced up the whole of San Diego, not just the park. That's why old timers remember who should get much of the credit when newcomers remark about the city's attractiveness.

She died on Easter Sunday, March 24, 1940, at a time when San Diego plants and flowers look their best.

Starting in probate and divorce cases, attorney Clara Shortridge Foltz later specialized in criminal law. In her eighties she ran unsuccessfully for governor.

Clara Shortridge Foltz:
California's first woman lawyer

Her opponent, upset about being outmaneuvered in the court-room, turned toward Clara Shortridge Foltz and muttered that a far better place for a woman would be at home raising children. The divorced mother of five, noted for her brevity, said, "A woman had better be in almost any business than raising men such as you."

Rejoinders like this were rare in a career that spanned more than half a century. She battled for the rights of women, prisoners and the poor in addition to practicing law. Attorney Oscar T. Shuck said of her, "She has become a favorite of the bar, whose leading members are pleased at all times to give her counsel."

The verbal jousting above occurred only a few years after she won admission to California's Bar in 1878, becoming the state's first woman attorney. Five years earlier the United States Supreme Court had denied a woman a license to practice law, saying, "The paramount destiny and mission of women are to fulfill the noble and benign offices of wife and mother."

Obstacles like this didn't faze the native of Henry County, Indiana. "I am descended from the heroic stock of Daniel Boone and never shrank from contest nor know a fear," she once said. At the age of fifteen she married Jeremiah D. Foltz, moved to Illinois, gave birth to five children and found time to teach school as well. The family moved to California when she was twenty-five. Two years later she divorced Jeremiah Foltz.

Two of her three brothers practiced law and gave her moral support when she began to read law in the San Jose office of Judge C. C. Stephens. Candidates for the bar exam prepared in this manner prior to the proliferation of law schools. A problem existed, however, in California's Code of Civil Procedure, which declared that the only people who could become attorneys were "any white male citizen" with suitable morals and knowledge. She rewrote that portion of the code, changing the phrase to "any citizen or person" and began persuading legislators to amend the law.

She convinced friends and strangers to write solons on the issue. The measure became known as the "Woman Lawyer's Bill," but her

Foltz's early advocacy and leadership helped these San Diego women win the right to vote in 1911. The nation followed suit, but not until 1920, about 100 years after the suffragette movement started in America.

change in the wording also would open the door for all minorities who had been excluded. Nettled by the legislators who preferred the status quo, she described them as "narrow-guage statesmen who grew red as turkey gobblers mouthing their ignorance against the bill." In 1876 the California Legislature passed the bill. Two years later she began practicing in San Jose and handled mostly divorce and probate matters.

Foltz saw the need for formal schooling so she applied at Hastings Law School in San Francisco. The school turned her down. Only males were permitted, she learned. She sued and won the right to attend, and the California Supreme Court upheld the verdict. Today, the school's Women's Union is named in her honor.

In 1887 she moved to San Diego where she established a law practice and became editor and publisher of the *San Diego Bee*, a new daily. Historian William Smythe described it as a lively journal. The *San Diego Union* acquired the paper two years after its beginning. Foltz moved to Los Angeles and became the first woman deputy district attorney in the United States.

"Though Foltz did some probate and divorce law, she preferred to practice criminal law," said Helen Rowe, an attorney and historian of the San Diego Bar, in a 1986 profile. "Foltz became an innovative, zealous, persistent advocate of penal reform. She lobbied for segregation of juvenile and adult inmates. She fought for the removal of iron cages in San Francisco courtrooms that housed inmates during their trials. She championed the creation of California's first system of inmate parole."

She believed poor people deserved the services of skilled, experienced counsel when accused of crimes. It took nearly twenty-five years of argument and persuasion until California lawmakers passed the "Foltz-(Public) Defender Bill" in 1921.

Described as "one of the personable and noteworthy suffragettes"—women who campaigned for their right to vote in federal elections—Foltz headed their state league several years. During her San Diego stay she presided over the local Nationalist Club, formed during a short-lived movement to socialize basic

industry. Many supported it in California where the Southern
Pacific Railroad virtually ran the state for a while.

Another state law she drafted enabled qualified women to hold
jobs as public administrators, notaries public and executors of
estates. She taught law and ran for the post of governor when she
was eighty-one, still advocating the rights of women.

Her colleague Oscar Shuck, in the book *Bench and Bar*, also saw
Foltz as " . . . self reliant, her argument is terse and condensed, her
speech fluent. Having a good voice, engaging manners, and dressing with excellent taste, displaying constant evidence of strict and
careful parental training, and always wearing the jewel of true
womanhood, she has become a favorite."

She would also be a favorite with poor people accused of crimes
today, if they knew about her. An annual Clara Shortridge Foltz
Award for outstanding legal services to needy criminal defendants
was created in 1985 by the American Bar Association, the State Bar
of California and various local bar associations in the state.

John D. Spreckels:
Midas with a yen for jokes

The jokes that San Diego's wealthiest man played on his staff and associates leaned toward the risque, so his biographer H. Austin Adams back in the circumspect days of 1924 didn't include many samples in *The Man John D. Spreckels*. But he described how the victims got even on Spreckels' sixty-fifth birthday:

Members of Spreckels' corporate executive committee commissioned a respected artist, Arthur Cahill, to paint two portraits of the boss standing by a table. They did not tell their committee chairman about the second version. So after the birthday party dining, while the cigars were still aglow, the chairman called Spreckels forward, extolled the man and unveiled the masterpiece. Glaring out at the crowd was a bloated old soak, an oversized stogie in one hand. The chairman, for a change, was speechless. He wilted into a chair. Spreckels glowered. Not until tiny lights began twinkling in the garish tie clasp and the huge diamond ring did he begin guffawing and the crowd followed suit. Then the other portrait was presented, revealing a formal, imposing man.

By that point in his life, John Diedrich Spreckels, in addition to his Coronado mansion on Glorietta Boulevard, owned and operated at various times:

The Hotel del Coronado
North Island
San Diego-Coronado Ferry System
San Diego & Arizona Railway
San Diego Electric Railway
Union-Tribune Publishing Company
Belmont Park in Mission Beach
Two downtown office buildings bearing his name.

Except for a fluke, Spreckels might never have set foot in San Diego. On a cruise from San Francisco, his schooner ran low on supplies and docked in San Diego Bay. A properly impressed citizenry greeted him. He in turn seemed impressed by the real estate boom still at fever pitch in July, 1887 and accepted an offer for a coal-handling wharf franchise. As word got out about this impending deal, prices for lots zoomed even higher.

Spreckels was tough. He, his sister Emma and brothers Claus, Jr., Adolph and Gus were the only ones of eleven children to reach adulthood as smallpox and other childhood maladies took their toll. The growing up credo, "Work, not talk," came from Claus, Sr., who had arrived in New York, broke, at the age of seventeen, taught himself the secrets of sugar refining and became Hawaii's "Sugar King."

John finished up his schooling in Hanover, Germany, where boxing and fencing were studied along with chemistry and engineering. When his father heard that John was scheduled to fight a duel over a young woman's honor, he called the student home and employed him as a refinery laborer. John worked his way up until he accumulated enough money and a line of credit to build a schooner with a five-hundred ton displacement. He next signed a cargo contract with his father, but not until the son cut rates below the competition. Soon he owned a fleet of nine ships for his general shipping and import business that made him a millionaire even while still working for his father.

In 1877 he married Lillie Siebein in Hoboken. They lived first in Hawaii, then San Francisco. When lawlessness prevailed, Spreckels helped organize the vigilantes and issued rifles to one-

Sunning, special events, study and get-togethers occur at the Spreckels Organ Pavilion in between the 2 p.m. Sunday concerts held each month except February.

hundred of the men on his payroll. He led the drills for them in the refinery yard.

San Francisco remained home base until the earthquake of 1906 persuaded the Spreckels that San Diego's climate, opportunity and distance from the San Andreas fault might be healthier for the couple and their four children. John Spreckels bought an eight-block square section of the downtown area and built a million dollar theater. His numerous donations included the Balboa Park organ pavilion that bears his name. At one juncture, he paid ten percent of all property taxes in San Diego County.

One of his biggest contributions began as a profit-making enterprise. He invested six million dollars to form the San Diego &

Arizona Railroad in 1905. Thirteen years and twelve million additional dollars later the "Impossible Railroad" made it to Campo and down the tortuous Carriso Gorge for the long-awaited railroad connection with the East. The construction frustrations, plus the time and money, explained the reluctance of other rail-

When the Number One San Diego & Arizona train came to Campo, the celebrants included, from left, John F. Forward, Sr., San Diego's mayor in 1909 when ground was broken; John D. Spreckels; and two early Campo settlers—Alphonso Grigsby and "Uncle" Lee Morris.

road interests to undertake the project, said James R. Mills in *San Diego: Where California Began.*

While John was a child his father taught him that anything worth having must be worth working for. This influenced him to try a prank the family always remembered. Seances and the mystical work of mediums intrigued the nation while he was in his teens. One day his mother and Emma became curious when a roll of darning cotton popped out of their basket and rolled out of reach. The next day, another roll hopped out and the basket tipped over. In the week that followed eyes widened as doors opened and closed untouched by human hands. Chairs jiggled as people prepared to sit down. On the day that a rocking horse pranced in the hallway, John's father, a pragmatic type, investigated and found a black thread leading into the lad's room. There a multitude of threads led into the closet where he discovered John in his mischief control center. The father broke into laughter and a relieved son joined in.

The jokes, a delight in playing the piano and a warm family relationship were aspects of the tycoon the public rarely saw, according to the biography by Austin Adams. The stern-visaged John Diedrich Spreckels was more often regarded as the midas who owned a piece of almost every action in town. He died in 1926 at the age of seventy-three.

San Diego Zoo's Belle Benchley introduced a hospital, natural habitats, wildlife conservation, research and public education years ahead of other zoos.

Belle J. Benchley:
The chameleon-like zoo chief

Starting at about the age of six, Belle Jennings would meander away from her ranch home and find a favorite observation post. She chattered with the rabbits, squirrels, birds and an occasional snake, but not until she had completed a getting acquainted ritual.

"I preferred to sit quietly watching the Point Loma animals, which like children, prefer to make all the advances," she said in the first of four books she wrote, *My Life in a Manmade Jungle.*

It was as though she blended into the landscape near Canon Road. Through the years she continued to change, developing as a homemaker, mother and an executive. Her comparison of animals with children furnishes a clue to her acclaim later as director of the San Diego Zoo. She insisted that a zoo's success hinges on the health and vigor of the animals. In her estimation, zoo visitors rated as VIPs, yet definitely came behind the permanent guests.

When she was five, Belle's parents had moved to Point Loma in 1887 from Larned, a central Kansas town encircled by communities such as Pawnee Rock, Radium, Zook and Frizell. Her father, Fred M. Jennings, became San Diego County sheriff. Belle attended a one room Roseville school house. Her sister Orrell Jane and brother Frank also had been born in Kansas. Five more brothers and sisters made their appearances in Point Loma.

She earned a teaching certificate from San Diego State Normal School. For three years she taught Pala Indian youngsters on the reservation northeast of San Diego, then met and married William

L. Benchley in 1906. They settled in Fullerton where a son Edward was born. This led to her interest in school affairs; she became the city's first woman school trustee, serving from 1919 to 1924. The following year the Benchleys divorced and she returned to San Diego with Edward.

While waiting for word about her job application for the Port Commission, Benchley received a telephone call in 1925 from Dr. Harry Wegeforth, the man who almost single-handidly created and nurtured the zoo in between caring for his patients. Could she help temporarily while the zoo's bookkeeper went on vacation? he asked. She agreed.

In no time at all she discovered the job exceeded the keeping of books. She pinch hit at the gate, collecting the dime admission. She cajoled donors for a bit more giving before payday. She became Florence Nightengale for the ailing monkey or zebra, and fed the birds.

What started as a temporary assignment became full time. In just two years Dr. Wegeforth saw that she was promoted to the top staff position—executive secretary. This made her the ranking woman employee in the county. Later her title would more accurately be changed to director, the first woman in the world to head a major zoo.

The city finally loosened its purse strings in 1928, allocating $36,000 for the zoo's operation. It wasn't until 1934 that the citizens voted to tax themselves two cents per hundred dollars valuation for zoo funding. The ballot measure had passed three times before, then was kicked out on technical grounds.

Belle Jennings Benchley possessed the courage and tenacity that innovators require if their ideas are to blossom. She helped start a tour program for all the second grade students in the county in 1926. She inaugurated the first zoo hospital in the United States in 1929. She could convey her feelings about the zoo's educational and entertainment values, so a seemingly constant round of talks began for service clubs and other groups. She took small animals with her on these speaking engagements, a practice TV talk shows appreciated and adopted in a later generation.

Benchley and Dr. Wegeforth argued long and hard sometimes about priorities and improvements. Let a word of criticism surface about one of them, however, and the other stood up in defense.

Benchley lost an unusually dedicated ally when the doctor died in 1941. If anyone questioned her leadership ability with him gone, they were answered by the zoo's growing attendance figures and worldwide acclaim. By the time she retired in 1953, attendance had more than quadrupled in the years she served as director. By the 1980s, the number of visitors was exceeding thirty million people a year.

At her retirement party, grateful citizens pitched in for a special gift — an around the world trip. In presenting the news, business leader Laurence M. Klauber concluded:
"And when you sail upon the Nile
The hippo and the crocodile
Had better climb a tree,
Or shipped aboard a modern ark
They'll land in this Balboa Park
For all our kids to see."

In 1963 she was informed that the zoo's governing body, the Zoological Society of San Diego, had named an expanse of the Bird and Great Ape Mesa the Belle Benchley Plaza. She was acclaimed San Diego's outstanding citizen in 1969, the same year that the Belle Benchley Primary School was dedicated. She died on December 17, 1973.

Captain Henry Fitch and Josefa Carrillo:
Love conquers all

Captain Henry Fitch dipped his anchor in San Diego Bay in 1826. He was not the first United States citizen to do so. Captain Charles Winship aboard the *Betsy* beat him by twenty-six years. Nor was Fitch the first American to wed a Mexican maiden in California. However, the captain and Josefa Carrillo in 1829 achieved an enduring measure of fame by being the first American and senorita to elope.

Today's parents, especially cost-conscious ones, may promote elopement, but in the early 1800s it was one of those unthinkable acts. It was contrary to custom and church dictates.

Henry Delano Fitch, a man with pleasant appearance and initiative, had met his beloved soon after his first San Diego visit. Josefa, then fifteen years of age, quickly fell for the gringo with the pleasant manners. They courted under watchful eyes of chaperones at fandangos, picnics, feasts, bull fights and the holidays her people arranged with a frequency that would delight a greeting card sales person.

Within a year the captain declared his intentions and obtained approval from Don Joaquin Carrillo, father of Josefa, who was impressed by the suitor's enterprise in opening a local mercantile store. Fitch joined the Catholic Church and became a citizen of Mexico. He even acquired a new moniker: Enrique Domingo Fitch.

Governor Jose Maria Echeandía, with headquarters in San Diego, hoped one day Josefa might be his, according to some accounts. This might explain why the wedding party gathered April 14 at the Carrillo ranch instead of the church where the governor could call it off. So Padre Antonio Menendez began the ceremony before a house filled with relatives and friends.

A career-minded Domingo Carrillo, Echeandía's adjutant general, interrupted the ceremony by hollering, "Halt. I refuse to be a witness to this." Which was all it took then to put a wedding on hold.

Fitch fretted. Josefa sobbed. Much discussion followed. Finally Father Menendez whispered an alternative in Fitch's ear — get married in another country.

Then in a bold act that would endear her to contemporary soap opera fans, she said, "Why don't you carry me off, Don Enrique?" Thus with an idea from the padre and an appeal from his fiancée, Fitch wasted no more time. He told Pio Pico, Josefa's cousin, about the proposed solutions to the impasse. Another confidante, Captain Barry, said his ship the *Vulture* was hoisting anchor that very night. Fitch should join him at once in boarding her and a boat would be sent ashore for Josefa at dusk, Barry said. Pico offered to deliver the maiden, which he did by horseback. The *Vulture* swooped out of sight under cover of darkness.

Don Joaquin Carrillo ranted. His wife worried. The church hierarchy and most of Southern California could not believe it. Soon after the *Vulture* docked in Valpairiso, Chili, the lovers completed their vows. They returned more than a year later, bringing with them a marriage certificate and their first born, Enrique Eduardo.

With much pleading, Josefa obtained her father's forgiveness, although he remained upset with the captain. The ecclesiastical judge for the territory, Padre Jose Sanches, called for an investigation. He decreed that Fitch must appear in San Gabriel "on most serious charges" of marriage ceremony rule infractions. Instead, the captain sent a courier with the marriage certificate and sailed

*When Henry Fitch took the oath as a Mexican citizen he became Enrique Domingo
Fitch, but his name was mud· after eloping with Josefa Carrillo in 1829.*

northward. Padre Sanches found a willing ally in the governor, who ordered Fitch's arrest. Collared in Monterey, he returned under guard to San Gabriel's presidio. Josefa was ordered to remain under custody.

After charges, denials and counter charges, the judge freed the Fitches, but only on the condition they perform acts of penance and Fitch, the chief instigator, donate a bell weighing at least fifty pounds, to the church in Los Angeles.

Time soothed Don Carrillo's tempest, Fitch's San Diego store prospered, Josefa gave birth to eleven children, including one named Josefa, and in 1841 Governor Manuel Micheltorena presented the Fitchs with a land grant for a rancho near Sonoma. One imagines, if this were given soap opera treatment, a closing scene from a church tower with a bell — the captain's, of course — pealing sonorously.

Agoston Haraszthy:
The unlucky innovator

It looked like a blatant case of a public servant at the trough. Sheriff Agoston Haraszthy's bid of $5,000 exceeded the low bid by $2,000, yet he won the job of building San Diego's first jail in 1851. Some people probably thought his being sheriff influenced the decision. Others surely suspected that nepotism prevailed since Haraszthy's father served as board of trustees chairman.

The curious aspect of the project was why anyone wanted the job in the first place. The city's treasury amounted to $10,600 when it incorporated in 1850, but that had dwindled. Nonethess, Haraszthy hired Daniel B. Kurtz as his contractor. Kurtz set the cobbles in mortar, then forgot or ignored the cement. A downpour damaged the project before the wood roof went on, so Haraszthy sought another $2,000 or else a contract cancellation. He agreed to accept subscription receipts, or scrip, in lieu of payment.

Today, city officials cringe at the idea of someone finding any of the one-hundred dollar scrip certificates because they bear an interest rate of eight percent a month. It's a possibility; Haraszthy and other scrip holders did not get paid.

The twenty-by-fifty-foot jail pleased prisoners, if no one else. The first man incarcerated, Roy Bean, poked with his knife and with about as much difficulty as carving a hole in a fresh donut he opened an escape hatch. Once outside he headed for the nearest bar.

Haraszthy ended up the goat as far as San Diegans were concerned and Kurtz, who should bear some of the scorn, it seems, went on to become mayor and a state senator. This sort of luck proved typical for Haraszthy throughout the rest of his days. Despite it all he would achieve renown as the Father of California Viticulture.

A count in his native Hungary, Haraszthy reached San Diego in 1849 at the age of thirty-seven. He dreamed of growing grapes that equalled the family's best in Europe. He bought land and planted cuttings. After winning the public's pardon for the jail fiasco, voters elected him state assemblyman. He proposed one bold step: split California into two states. That would halt the benefits Northern Californians enjoyed from high taxes paid by people down south.

His trips to the legislature persuaded him that the Haraszthy family should move north, closer to the climate grapes prefer. They did, first near Mission Dolores in San Francisco and later to Crystal Springs in San Mateo County, where he divided his time between viticulture and an assignment as an assayer, melter and refiner at the San Francisco Mint.

In 1857, two years after the United States Treasury hired his firm, he was charged with embezzling $151,000 worth of gold from the mint. The case dragged on four years until he could prove his theory about the missing metal. Soot and grime taken from roofs of nearby buildings sparkled with gold particles, which literally flew up the chimneys. The culprit? Blowers, installed to furnish the mint's furnaces with a proper draft.

Meanwhile, General Mariano Guadalupe Vallejo introduced Haraszthy to the near-perfect vine growing conditions of the Sonoma area and there the count established his Buena Vista vineyard in 1857. Soon his wines were winning top State Fair prizes. His neighbors experienced problems, however, caused by inferior vines and their ignorance.

"The state should appoint a commission to collect the best varieties of vines and fruit trees and study the methods used in Europe," he suggested to the legislature, which endorsed the idea and named him one of the three commissioners. The legislators

A sort of "Johnny Appleseed of grapes," Agoston Haraszthy came to the San Diego area from Wisconsin late in 1849. He saw the potential of planting vines brought directly from Europe but the Southern California climate proved too warm.

Early vineyards lacked premium grapes; Haraszthy's barnstorming trip solved that.

Fancy footwork was one of the requisites for employment in the old wineries.

appropriated no money for the fact-gathering sojourn, but the count went anyway, confident the lawmakers would pay him back later.

When he came back, after spending more than $10,000 for 100,000 vines, the Civil War had turned the lawmakers into skeptics, especially of someone from San Diego, a place they knew was infested with "copperheads"—people sympathetic to the South. The lawmakers pigeonholed the bill for his expenses and also reneged on funds needed to distribute his collection. Those cuttings could have "endowed California with the fruit of 2,000 years of European grape growing," as one writer put it.

Stung but undaunted, the tall, polished count journeyed about the state in 1862 selling growers the vines for whatever their savings allowed and imparting what he'd learned. It proved a hit or miss outing, but it laid the groundwork for a flourishing California wine industry.

Haraszthy showed the growers that vines need not be next to streams; in fact they grew better when not irrigated. He pioneered the use of redwood for storage casks when oak prices rose. He sent cuttings of his vines statewide and sold thousands of rooted vines. He wrote a book and articles, sharing his know-how.

A few years later, William C. Ralston, founder and head of the Bank of California, persuaded Haraszthy to incorporate the Buena Vista vineyard, which the count had heavily mortgaged to finance expansion. Ralston's push for quick profits and other problems pressured the count into resigning in 1866.

Haraszthy headed for Nicaragua, lured by the reports of its untapped resources. He developed a sugar plantation and a rum distillery.

On a solo trip to the interior, Haraszthy apaparently tried to cross a wide stream on a tree branch. Nearby, a few days earlier, an alligator had dragged a cow into the water from the bank. When the count did not return, members of a search party spotted a single set of footprints to the tree and a broken branch. They concluded that—if he was lucky—he had drowned.

Count Haraszthy's ingenuity and enterprise provided a robust legacy. The $10,000 he risked led to retail sales of California wine measured today in billions of dollars per year.

A millionaire at the age of 28, merchant and sea captain William Heath "Kanaka Bill" Davis visited San Diego for his health, but his economic well being suffered.

William Heath Davis:
The distracted developer

"A s a trader** and sea captain, Mr. Davis, you can appreciate
the value of this splendid harbor. What's more, with California soon to become part of the Union, we will see a westward
migration of people seeking the benefits of this climate and the
opportunites for trade."

It's easy to imagine Lieutenant Andrew B. Gray employing
expansive gestures with this sort of message in February, 1850. The
United States Boundary Commission engineer and surveyor put
into words what William Heath "Kanaka Bill" Davis already knew.
Gold Rush fever already had warmed up San Diego. And Davis'
own health had improved during his vacation from operating a San
Francisco store that made him a millionaire at the age of twenty-
eight.

Gray convinced Davis, who put up most of the $2,304 needed for
a one-hundred and sixty acre waterfront parcel bounded by today's
Front Street and Broadway. They brought in three local men and
formed a consortium to build and promote New Town. It consisted
of fifty-six blocks. Davis contracted for a shipload of lumber,
including half a dozen pre-fabricated buildings that arrived in San
Francisco from Portland, Maine. He built a wharf and warehouse
for $60,000 at the foot of Market Street and drafted plans for a
coaling station. A little lobbying, plus the gift of the required
amount of land, brought an Army supply depot and barracks, with
the prospect of a base later.

By the end of 1850 New Town boasted three stores, a lumber

yard, two small hotels and a few homes. Ultimately, the number of residents would peak at two-hundred and fifty, then head downhill.

What went wrong? John R. Bartlett of the U. S. Boundary Commission stated it concisely early in 1852: "There is no business to bring vessels here, except an occasional one with government stores. There is no water nearer than the San Diego River, three miles distant . . . wood has to be brought some eight or ten miles; nor is there any arable land within four miles."

The Army reconsidered on building its post in New Town. The government declined on establishing a customshouse or a post office. Rumors of Indian rebellions scared prospective settlers. Topping things off, one of San Francisco's frequent fires torched Davis' store; he lost $700,000.

Davis did not grasp what New Town needed nor what he should do to make it succeed, according to Andrew F. Rolle in *An American in California*. At critical times Davis spent his days hunting gold or pursuing other interests instead of overseeing matters in San Diego. During a drain on his cash reserves, he sold properties in the northern part of the state for about one-tenth of their market value. By the time Alonzo Horton arrived on the scene in 1867, New Town was known as Davis' Folly. In what had become a typical result, Horton bought a lot with a small building from Davis for one-hundred dollars, then resold it for $1,000 to a man who converted it into a hotel.

Kanaka Bill was born in Hawaii, the grandson of Oliver Holmes, who married a Polynesian princess, Mahi, and later became Oahu's governor. Captain William H. Davis, Sr., married Holmes' daughter who gave birth to William, Jr., in 1821. The boy's father died. His stepfather, John Coffin Jones, also was a seafarer. Young Davis accompanied him on voyages to Alaska, then, when he was ten, to California.

After sporadic school studies, he came under the wing of an uncle, Nathan Spear, a wealthy merchant with stores in San Francisco and Monterey. As his protege, Kanaka Bill learned

The William Heath Davis House, one of six pre-fabricated buildings shipped from Maine in 1849, now can be visited in its restored state at Fourth and Island in San Diego. It was part of "New Town" or "Davis' Folly," as it was later called.

merchandising and sea faring, including the smuggling that traders regularly practiced to escape tariffs that ran as high as one-hundred percent of a ship cargo's worth.

Davis married Maria de Jesus Estudillo of San Leandro in 1847, served for a short time on San Francisco's town council and joined the vigilantes. In the lean years following the San Diego fiasco, he jotted down his recollections. The manuscript was lost or taken after the 1906 earthquake in San Francisco. His children saved his notes, however, and twenty years after his death they gave the set to John Howells who published it as *Seventy-five Years in California*.

It was a seventy-five year period that brings to mind a Chinese saying: "The larger the fortune hoarded, the greater the loss. The higher the climb, the quicker the fall."*

* From *A Chinese Garden of Serenity* published by The Peter Pauper Press and translated by Chao Tze-chiang.

This 1858 photograph by J. Henfield is believed to the first ever taken of Old Town, according to James R. Mills in his book San Diego: Where California Began.

Alonzo Erastus Horton:
San Diego's father

"I'm getting tired of handling so much money."
Alonzo Erastus Horton reportedly made this statement while selling the two-hundred and twenty-six blocks of what is now downtown San Diego. And no wonder. His outlay for eight-hundred acres purchased at an auction in 1867 totaled only thirty-three cents an acre. Two years later he paid $4,000 for a one-hundred and sixty acre parcel needed to sew up the section known as the Horton Addition.

These figures surfaced in research by Dr. Robert F. Heilbron. Other historians have credited Horton with a twenty-seven cents per acre figure.

Horton started something big and it was fueled in 1885 by the resumption of railroad service to an eastward connection. "San Diego became real estate mad," according to the Federal Writers' Project book *San Diego: A California City.* "People lived in tents on their lots until they could clear away the brush and cactus. More frequently they sold out at fancy prices before they could settle on the land. Buyers bought from maps without inspecting the purchase, and in turn sold to other speculators sight unseen."

Local people jumped on the bandwagon. Housewives, lawyers, clerks, ministers, maids and businesssmen began buying and sell-

Posing with his second wife, "Babe," (for Sara Wilson Babe), Alonzo Horton once revealed his mettle on a trip East. After Panama natives attacked the ship's passengers, he kept revolvers smoking as he led his companions back to their ship.

ing. Some speculators paid as much as five-hundred dollars for a place in line to buy property.

This became the first peak in a real estate roller coaster ride that first delighted then devastated speculators on at least three occasions between the 1867 birth of the Horton Addition and 1906. Horton counted the greenbacks, then invested in more land or new ventures. He gave lots to the Methodists, Episcopalians and Baptists for new churches. He donated land to people who pledged to build houses at once. He donated the site for the proposed courthouse. Sometimes he paid his employees with property.

Some businessmen called him "Corner Lot Horton." This term of derision came from his practice of offering smaller-than-normal corner parcels at prices twenty-five percent higher than lots next door, recalled Don M. Stewart in *Frontier Port*. The canny Horton, however, knew shop owners and some home buyers preferred the higher visibility on the corners. His new addition lacked alleys. People just used them for trash, Horton maintained, based on what he had seen in San Francisco and other cities, so he eliminated them.

Born in Connecticut in 1813, Horton moved near Lake Winnebago, Wisconsin, where almost single-handidly he created the city now known as Hortonville (pop. 2,000).

The lure of gold brought him West in 1849. He profited more from supplying ice and store merchandise in the Mother Lode than panning for the metal. He opened a San Francisco used furniture store, capitalizing on its booming population and the refurbishing needs caused by frequent fires. He foresaw even better returns in San Diego after hearing a speaker describe its climate, the harbor, the impact of a proposed railroad and the ample space for stores, homes and factories.

At the age of fifty-four he headed south on the steamer *Pacific*. Good downtown San Francisco lots then sold for $10,000 or more so Horton probably chortled when his bid of two-hundred and sixty-five dollars gave him title to those eight-hundred acres. But he also knew a major promotional effort must follow.

Horton returned to San Francisco. He gave maps, brochures

Opening of 100-room Horton House brought throngs in 1872. Despite all that hotel space, Horton kept his office under his hat.

and a spiel to anyone who appeared solvent and would listen. Hired runners helped spread the word and Horton collared anyone who showed some interest.

His efforts began paying off. In time tourists themselves helped. They returned home from Southern California with missionary zeal, buttonholing neighbors and writing newspapers about the American Riviera they had visited. Soon Horton could complain about handling all that money. He plowed it back: $45,000 for a new wharf at the end of Fifth Avenue; $150,000 for the one-hundred room Horton House.

Old timers scoffed at someone loony enough to build a hotel off the beaten track at what is now Third and Broadway with the business hub then at Fifth and Market. But Horton's hunch proved

San Diego Historical Society displays bust by Allen Hutchinson at Balboa Park Museum. San Diego Hardware has occupied two buildings of Lot C in Block 62 of Horton's Addition since 1892. The model wears nails, screw eyes, utensils, a butterfly hinge, padlock, nutmeg grater, scissors, tin drinking cup, various chains and a mini cast iron stove—all of which the store presently handles.

right. He helped start the first library by swapping a downtown lot for books from historian Hubert H. Bancroft.

A lifelong Republican, Horton decreed that only bonafide supporters would be on his payroll. Party conversions occurred whenever real estate booms began and he hired more workers, because the town leaned toward Democratic policies. His contemporaries regarded Horton as an honest and crackerjack, if somewhat eccentric, promoter, but an ineffectual businessman, according to Don Stewart, a former councilman, Postmaster and Democratic Party leader, who was born in San Diego six years after Horton arrived. When real estate values dropped, Horton lost most of the money he had tired of counting. The bank he founded, the hotel and other enterprises passed into the control of others.

Most people regard Horton as the father of San Diego. Others point to Juan Cabrillo who was the first to discover San Diego Bay in 1542. Some nominate Junipero Serra, the padre who guided the establishment of Alta California's first mission in 1769. William Heath Davis rates the "father" title, in Stewart's view. Davis was the catalyst for the 1850 development of New Town in the vicinity of today's Broadway, Front and the harbor. The project failed miserably.

Whatever Horton's parental ranking, he stands out as a herculean promoter who envisioned the metropolis San Diego one day would become. And he possessed the courage to act upon his vision.

Frank Kimball:
The frustrated railroad booster

The prospects in France looked — magnifique. Tom Scott, head of the newly organized Texas & Pacifc Railroad, had arranged a meeting with some Paris financiers during the week of September 8, 1873. They expressed interest in a $54 million bond issue for a proposed railroad line linking the San Diego area to the East. Scott had obtained federal grants worth nearly $70 million the previous year and begun roadbed construction.

But during the week, Scott scooted across the channel for a London sightseeing interlude. Meanwhile the Paris moneymen sought his whereabouts, ready to deal. They changed their minds on "Black Friday," the thirteenth, when the New York stock market nose dived.

This quirky timing epitomized the luck San Diego and National City experienced whenever they tried snagging a railroad connection. With fine harbor facilities close by, regular train service could mean profitable trade with China, Japan and other Pacific Rim countries. Otherwise, Los Angeles and San Francisco surely would capture most of the business. For Frank Kimball and his brothers Warren and Levi, a railroad promised more National City settlers and tourists, which in turn meant more real estate sales and a demand for their farm crops.

To exacerbate matters, railroad barons proved cunning at best and downright dishonest at the other extreme. Scott, for example, reneged earlier in the year on a deal with Frank Kimball to establish shops and a depot in National City, causing an exodus of about half the residents.

Frank, with help from his brothers, kept plugging. As the area's spokesman he visited railroad moguls back East. He finally ended up with an Atchinson, Topeka & Santa Fe Railroad agreement for a connecting line from San Diego to Colton, just outside San Bernardino. In exchange, the railroad got 17,000 acres of land, including some of the Kimball brothers' choice waterfront property, and $25,000 in cash. Frank Kimball also negotiated a deal with Santa Fe, persuading the company to build its shops and freight station office in National City. This tempered the joy San Diegans first felt

FIRST PASSENGER
TRAIN OF THE CALIFORNIA SOUTHERN RAILROAD

Chartered on October 12, 1880, the California Southern Railroad went into service between National City and Colton, near San Bernardino. Spring floods of 1884 washed out the Temécula Canyon track, which was built too near the river bed.

With brothers Levi and Warren, Frank Kimball founded National City after they came from the San Francisco area in 1868. They paid $1.13 each for 26,632 acres.

about the news that at last a railroad was on the way.

In August, 1882 the one-hundred and twenty-seven mile section of line went into service under the aegis of the California Southern Railroad, on which Kimball served as a board member. The route's Temécula Canyon portion washed out in an 1884 flood. When train service was reestablished in 1885, business boomed. Speculators arrived on the heels of settlers in a real estate buying orgy that lasted until the spring of 1888.

As business slumped, the financially troubled Santa Fe transferred its shops and freight office to San Bernardino, causing Kimball to observe: "It has every appearance of an ingeniously planned scheme, which only experts could plan, to secure a vast waterfront adapted to railroad purposes, with no intention of using it, but rather prevent anyone else from using it."

Frank and his brothers came West in 1861 from their Contoocook, New Hampshire birthplace. With their carpentry skills they built a thriving building contracting business in the San Francisco area. Frank, the youngest, needed a change in climate for his health. He first considered the Los Angeles area, then found the Rancho de la Nacio for sale a few miles south of San Diego. The Kimball trio bought the 26,632-acre spread for $30,000 in 1868. Taking a leaf from Alonzo Horton's book, the brothers laid out a subdivision. Without a rail connection or an ample water supply, however, lot sales lagged, although in the following year Frank sold some choice sites for seventeen dollars per acre.

Amidst real estate deals he ordered seeds from San Francisco and Hawaii and planted lemons, figs, grapes, olives and vegetables. The Kimballs created a water company. They secured rights to Sweetwater River water and Frank spotted a funnel-spout section of the canyon ideally suited for a dam.

He sparked operations of the first San Diego County railway which served Nestor, Palm City and Otay from a San Diego terminal. In its heyday, one-hundred and twenty-six units, many of them one and two car trains, made the rounds.

In 1886 the Santa Fe's subsidiary, San Diego Land and Town Company, started work on the Sweetwater Dam and completed it in April two years later. Said Richard F. Pourade in *The Glory Years*, "For Frank Kimball it was the high moment of the long struggle which had taken so many years and absorbed much of his land and wealth."

Some of his money helped start an Otay watch works. It failed. He experimented with a shipment of 1,000 oysters, which he dumped into the bay fed by the Sweetwater. It, too, failed. He opened a United States Department of Agriculture experimental station in 1888. All of which suggests he willingly tried almost anything that might spur business and attract newcomers.

Like Alonzo Horton, Ephraim Morse and other area entrepreneurs, Frank Kimball ended up broke, dragged down by an economic depression rather than his venturesome spirit. His brother Warren, who also became wealthy with his planing mill and other enterprises, also ended up almost penniless. The financial tailspin broke up what had been a long and satisfying relationship.

Frank Kimball died in 1913. Like the Russian proverb, "He went for wool and came home shorn," especially in dealings with the railroads.

A Norman castle inspired Elisha Babcock's concept for Hotel del Coronado. It opened in 1888, complete with its own power plant. Daily $3 rate included meals.

Tent City, which included thatched huts, attracted tourists in 1904. They enjoyed swimming, boating, strolling and band concerts on the Silver Strand.

Hotel builder in a hurry

S ome people, inspired by a big idea, prefer a process of mulling, digesting, pondering—and often end up on a one-way track into inertia. Not so with Elisha Spurr Babcock, Jr., at least when it came to building the Hotel del Coronado.

His doctor had sent him West in 1884 for rest and recuperation--- the standard tuberculosis prescription then. Babcock, thirty-four years of age, settled in San Diego along with Hampton L. Story, a member of a Chicago family that prospered from the manufacture of pianos.

The two men often rowed a boat across the bay to a sandy patch of what was known in those days as the San Diego Peninsula. Babcock's wife Isabel observed: "When Elisha found that all he had to do in order to get well was to catch four-pound sea perch in the Pacific Ocean and hunt rabbits on the peninsula of San Diego, he decided this was the place for us to live."

His Evansville, Indiana, civil engineering training and railroad investments had helped Babcock accumulate a comfortable boodle. Story also was well fixed. One summer day in 1885, after returning from a pursuit of rabbits, Babcock said, "We ought to build a hotel, Story, the brightest . . . smartest hostelry on any coast . . . We ought to build it on that spot across the bay where we sunburned this morning." Story reportedly heaved a sigh as if to say, *This old-timer doesn't need any new worlds to conquer.* But as Babcock's enthusiasm grew, Story, mindful of the real estate deals percolating in town, soon began seeing dollar signs flashing where only rabbits had hopped before.

Babcock's plan possessed the simplicity of most good ideas. They formed a syndicate, bought the 4,185.46 acres of land, then began preparing for the sale of residential lots, which would raise the capital to build a hotel. Babcock knew a grand hotel spelled respectability for would-be home owners. As for an incoming supply of visitors, the railroads vied with each other, seeing which one could cut fares the most. The tariff eventually would end up at one dollar per head.

The combined Coronado (which means "crown") and North Island property cost $110,000. As soon as the tycoons signed the papers, land clearing began. Babcock hired almost every available able bodied man in town for daytime dirt moving and a brush roundup, helped by Henry Fenton's herd of 250 mules. At night the brush piles blazed, beacons of Babcock's urgency in clearing the way for the next day's work. By next spring Babcock and his associates had created the Coronado Beach Company.

Soon an advertising blitz swept the nation's major cities. People who bought a parcel and spent $1,000 immmproving it, the ads stated, would receive free water for one year and one-hundred and twenty local ferry and railway tickets. Inducements like these attracted more than 6,000 men, women and children to the first Coronado land auction on November 13, 1886. They squeezed onto ferry boats and almost anything else that floated. A band played. Refreshment booths abounded. Tents furnished a place to sit down in the shade.

San Diego attorney Levi Chase topped the bidding for the first lot with $1,600. Before sunset, he turned down an offer of from $400 to $2,000 more than he paid for it, depending on whose account one reads. Three hundred bidders spent $110,000 during the auction. Similar auctions in the weeks that followed brought in as much as $400,000 in one day. All told, nearly $2.2 million came in, enabling the sponsors to hold a hotel ground breaking in March 1887.

Harrison Gray Otis, publisher of the *Los Angeles Times*, said some home lot buyers kicked because, "In every deed a stipulation is inserted that no spirituous liquors shall ever be sold or drunk on the

Elisha Babcock

premises. People who want to get drunk must do so at the hotel."

Babcock lured the brothers James and Merritt Reid, Evansville architects, onto the staff with a vision of designing an Americanized castle in an incomparable setting. James Reid began his sketches, but Babcock couldn't wait. Work started on the basis of preliminary drawings and Reid never did find time for finished versions. Initially, North Island seemed the ideal spot. Its access problems, however, made the South Island's western shore the ultimate hotel site.

Construction challenges arose. Jobs across the bay kept carpenters busy, so Babcock boosted the pay scale. The three-dollars-per-day level drew a nucleus of journeymen from as far as

Chicago, although some took up real estate speculating instead of nail pounding. Those who hired on trained the novices. The Seven Companies in San Francisco sent 100 Chinese laborers.

". . . The hotel never did seem to stop growing," said Edward H. Davis, who came from his Mesa Grande ranch as a draftsman. "It was amazing how many rooms were built that were not even planned for at the start of construction."

Thomas A. Edison came from the East with advice on the installation of a generator. Originally, most rooms had fireplaces made from bricks formed out of clay found on the peninsula and baked in kilns next to the hotel site. A steam heating plant added in 1897 supplemented the fireplaces. By the official opening date of February 19, 1888, a total of 399 bedrooms were available. The theater and ballroom covered 111,000 square feet of floor space. Several guests had already signed in.

In a few months, though, San Diego's real estate boom turned to bust. John D. Spreckels, son of the "Sugar King," Claus Spreckels, first bought out Story, then paid Babcock more than one million dollars for his share and retained him as hotel manager and as an agent for other local business dealings.

Historian William E. Smythe said it was Babcock who first interested Spreckels in investing in San Diego enterprises, a move comparable in significance with the discovery of a downtown gold mine. Later Babcock and Spreckels experienced a falling out. The originator of the Hotel del Coronado ended up virtually bankrupt because of the impact of a 1916 flood on his businesses and the failure of his Western Salt Company, one of his major enterprises.

Ironically, the man who always seemed in a hurry had practically nothing left but time.

"The natural watering place of this whole Southern country" is how an auctioneer described the La Jolla landscape that Frank Botsford inspects.

Frank T. Botsford:
La Jolla's visionary founder

As developers go, Frank Terril Botsford couldn't match Alonzo Horton's promotional talents nor auctioneer Tom Fitch's flamboyant cajolery. But historians relish his role in founding La Jolla because this means they can feature that photograph of Botsford with the telescope. It's the ideal symbol of the search for prospects, profits, customers, a new era—almost anything. Which helps explain his title Father of La Jolla even though people settled there before him.

He had arrived in San Diego January 18, 1886 at the early stage of what would become the city's most frenetic real estate boom. Most of the people, according to historian Theodore S. Van Dyke, ". . . cared nothing about the solid resources of the land, and were looking only for amusement or a chance to make some money without work. For the news was already widely spread in the East that the land was 'booming' and it was more widely spread by the papers in all directions. There were still many who felt nothing but contempt for a country they did not understand . . . but the majority were on the other extreme and in finding the land rapidly growing, with crops all good and money plenty, fell at once into blind, unreasoning love with it."

After more than three decades of hopes, plans and disappointment, plus a devastating Temécula Canyon rail washout, a railroad finally existed with the Santa Fe's link to Colton, south of San Bernardino, up to Barstow then eastward or else west to Los Angeles. By spring of 1887 the fares from the Midwest would drop to as low as one dollar per person in a rate war between the railroads.

Botsford noted in his diary on March 16, 1886: "Magnificent day at La Jolla." The place made such an impression on him that on March 24 he bought it, despite the distance from the railroad and the lack of water. He sold one-fourth an interest to George W. Heald. Then came the search for the key resource — water. Week after week of probing passed. At last on February 4 of the next year he discovered water in the Rose Canyon area where he had purchased twenty acres.

Another quarter interest in the property was sold to Charles S. Dearborn and H. W. Whitney. The associates surveyed and subdivided their acreage, according to Howard S. F. Randolph in *La Jolla: Year By Year*. At a "La Jolla Park" auction at the end of April, C. A. Wetmore bid $1,250 for the first lot and other buyers put up or pledged $56,000 for other parcels. Throughout the region some people bought lots sight unseen. On occasion they acquired the bed of a river, the bay's bottom or inaccessible land. Of conditions in general, Van Dyke noted:

"Few people visited these additions to see what they were asked to invest in, but under the stimulus of band music and a free lunch, they bought from the auctioneer's map and made large payments down. In this way at least a quarter of a million dollars were thrown away upon alkali wastes, cobble-stone tracts, sand-overflowed

Gathering of sea moss at La Jolla's "Big Cave" attracts a clan after the years in which Frank Botsford's promotions popularized the area.

lands and cactus, the poorest land being usually put down on the townsite market."

Developers promised that new hotels, opera houses and bus lines would soon spring up in the often barren terrain. Wendell Eaton, one of the auctioneers for Babcock's consortium, advised prospects: "This is the natural watering place of this whole Southern country, and nothing can turn the tide from it. It is simply nature working . . . Today the property is as free as air, and you can buy it at your own price." He didn't fib. Some La Jolla view lots sold for under two-hundred dollars.

Historian William Smythe noted the boom's origin sprang from the railroad and improved public utilities, but emphasized the influence of a psychological effect. "The people were hypnotized," he wrote, "intoxicated, plunged into emotional insanity by the fact that they had unanimously and simultaneously discovered the ineffable charm of the San Diego climate . . . and the joy of life it implied."

The hitch, of course, "involved the prosaic matter of making a livelihood by some other means than exchanging real estate every few days at a profit," said Smythe.

San Diego swarmed with boomers who acquired farms, rangelands and unimproved, sand-swept acreage, then subdivided, tacked on fancy names and auctioned off the lots. Also swarming into the area were gamblers, crooks, prostitutes and entertainers along with the health seekers and well-heeled speculators during the tumultuous two-and-a-half years of the boom. Profligacy and vice entered into government, business and social life, said Walter Gifford Smith, historian.

The earliest settlers of La Jolla, brothers Daniel and Samuel Sizer, paid $1.25 per acre in 1869, then John Butler and F. Fredly followed suit. The long beach acquired notoriety; smugglers brought in Chinese laborers and opium.

In its formative years, La Jolla enjoyed a feeling of community, said Will Shaw, editor of the *La Jolla Journal*. On a birthday, anniversary or other special occasion, nearly the whole town joined in the celebration. When fishermen came in with a good catch, they shared it. A two-horse stage line furnished transportation. The water hauled in from Rose Canyon ended up in whiskey barrels until needed for domestic purposes.

All this began changing after Frank Botsford set up his tent. He began surveying the scene with a telescope and provided both the photographer and history aficionados with a memorable symbol.

Pio Pico:
California's last
Mexican governor

A t the age of twenty, Pio Pico traveled from his San Diego home to Los Angeles only to learn the alcalde, or town mayor, required visitors to present a passport.

"Right then and there I took paper and pen and forged a passport to which, at the bottom, I signed the name of the commander of San Diego, Captain Francisco Mariá Ruiz," Pico later told Thomas Savage, who was obtaining his recollections for historian Hubert H. Bancroft. "This I did because I knew Alcalde Avila would not discover it as he did not know how to read nor write."

Brash acts like this permeated the life of the last Mexican governor of California. In fact, Pico forged documents after his term of office ended, hoping he could acquire more land grants. This was recorded in attorney general Jeremiah Black's report to Congress following America's victory over Mexico in the war of 1846-48. If the United States had honored all of Pico's claims, the family would have owned 532,000 acres of prime land.

Born in the San Gabriel Mission in 1801, Pio grew up in San Diego. For several years after the death of his father, he operated a mercantile store there while his mother and sisters turned out fancy needlework. Even then the young man loved to gamble.

At the age of twenty-five he took on the mantle of a revolutionary, but the action traditionally resulted in comic opera theatrics. Opposing Mexican factions issued pompous declarations. Commanders drew battle lines far enough apart so hardly anyone died

Intrigues, revolts and feuds enlivened Pio Pico's path to the governor's post in 1845. He bested Manuel Micheltorena in gaining power.

from other than natural causes. Prisoners often turned out to be cousins or nephews and returned home with their captors.

The intrigues and revolutions may seem absurd until compared with, say, a neighboring country's civil war. On that basis, the Mexican modus operandi appears civilized. When the occasion demanded it, Mexican soldiers displayed skills that American General Stephen W. Kearny respected. He lost one-fifth of his dragoons to forces led by Pico's brother, Andrés. Kearny said that they were "admirably well mounted and the very best riders in the world; hardly one that is not fit for the circus."

In overall strength, though, the American forces, including settlers, outnumbered the Mexicans, which at their peak counted slightly more than three-hundred trained military men. The invaders capitalized on a split between Pio Pico, who had established his power base in Los Angeles, and military commandant José Castro headquarted in Monterey. Castro enjoyed a big edge over Pico; he controlled the troops and held the purse strings.

Pico had attained the governor's post in 1845, succeeding Manuel Micheltorena who had come to California with a motley crew, ostensibly soldiers, but made up of mostly paroled convicts; they gained notoriety by their inclination to pillage rather than protect the populus. Soon after Pico's appointment, he sent an aide to Mexico City with details on California's nonexistent military capabililty. The aide next visited Great Britain's admiral and told him Pico would place California under his protection if Mexico officials ignored the governor's dire situation.

The admiral, Pico said later, "was well disposed to the project." On his arrival, however, he "found the flag of the United States already flying over the territory and, of course, he did not have the opportunity to do anything."

After the war the short, stocky Pico delighted in dressing in his finest, medals covering his chest, on special occasions. He remained an habitual gambler. In the matter of a few minutes he lost $25,000 and three-hundred head of cattle when Jose Sepulveda's horse outraced his own. Many of Pico's friends and relatives lost their savings — money they lent him — when he could not pay off his

IOUs. At the age of sixty-eight he sold his ranch for $115,000, which he sank into the Pico House, the largest hotel of its day in Los Angeles. He signed away the deed for a short term loan of $65,000, unaware that the agreement pledged the property in case of a late payment. Pio Pico lived off friends and relatives until his death in 1894 at the age of ninety-three.

Among the water colors by seaman William Meyers during three years of voyaging is this view of the San Diego Presidio close to the time when Pio Pico served as governor.

A gentleman who wouldn't quit

"**H**e certainly gave us** the most graceful dancing that I had ever seen," Richard Henry Dana wrote of Don Juan Bandini in 1836. "He was dressed in white pantaloons, neatly made, a short jacket of dark silk gaily figured, white stockings and thin morocco slippers upon his very small feet."

The occasion was the Santa Barbara wedding of Senorita de la Guerra y Noriega and Alfred Robinson, one of the earliest United States settlers in the California region during the 1822-46 era of Mexican control. It was a laid-back, pleasure-bent period made possible economically by the sale of hides from cattle which proliferated after the missionaries brought them.

About one out of ten men could read and write. Indians performed most of the work. The women embroidered nearly every inch of cloth in the ranchos. They splurged aboard incoming ships that carried perfumes and shoes, silk sashes and shawls, woolens and utensils. These floating shopping centers then took on cattle hides for the return trip to Boston.

At the time of the wedding, Bandini was thirty-six. He had journeyed from Monterey to Santa Barbara aboard the ship on which Dana served as a seaman, an experience that led to *Two Years Before the Mast*. The book includes his first impression of the don:

"Among our passengers was a young man who was the best representation of a decayed gentleman I had ever seen. He was of the aristocracy of the country, his family being of pure Spanish blood. His father . . . having amassed a large property settled at

Unjustly labeled as the destroyer of missions, Don Juan Bandini never-theless profited by land grant gifts he later received. He supported the U. S. when the war began in 1846.

Flanked by homes of Alvorado, left, and Estudillo families was the showplace Casa de Bandini. Alfred L. Seeley bought it in 1869 and converted it into the Cos-mopolitan Hotel.

San Diego. His son was sent to Mexico where he received the best education and went into the first society of the capital. Misfortune, extravagance and want of funds soon ate the estate up, and Don Juan Bandini returned from Mexico accomplished, poor and proud, and without any office or occupation, to lead the life of most young men of the better families — dissolute and extravagant when the means were at hand."

That **combination** of being broke and and proud may explain why Bandini kept striving for goals beyond his grasp. He had served as a member of Mexico's assembly as a congressman, then vice president of a colonization company and California customs inspector. The colonization plan soured, however, and officials denied him his customs post. Adding insult to injury, they declared him guilty of smuggling. It was after these setbacks that Dana saw Don Juan Bandini as an example "of a decayed gentleman."

During Governor José Fegueroa's term, Bandini helped influence him to carry out the 1833 Secularization Act. The intent of the law was to return mission lands to the Indians and supplant the missionaries with secular church padres. Governor Figueroa finally acted despite misgivings about the Indians' ability to control their destinies, and with good reason. The missionaries treated them like retarded children.

Bandini's role earned him the title "Destroyer of the California Missions," but forces at work in Mexico and in California, spurred by the prospect of all that mission property up for grabs, clearly made the destruction more than a one man job.

A more accurate title for the don would be "The Revolution-ary." He played a role in the upheavals that have reminded most historians of comic operas. From 1831 to 1836 the California territory underwent eleven changes in governors. Three additional men appointed by Mexico were told to vamoose before they could assume the office.

Typically the "outs" issued a bombastic proclamation, then assembled between a dozen to one-hundred combatants and lobbed cannon balls at the "ins." Because brothers and fathers and sons often fought on opposite sides, the artillery set up just out of range; that way the same cannon balls could be used by both sides without casualties.

Bandini gained fringe benefits. His land grants included sections in today's Riverside and San Bernardino counties as well as a part of Baja California. He profited from cattle hide sales and from a San Diego store he established. During 1845-46 he served as Governor Pio Pico's secretary of state.

After the 1846 outbreak of the United States-Mexico war, he risked his life by siding with the Yankees. One of his daughters reportedly hoisted a homemade American flag on the plaza pole as a greeting for the bedraggled, seasick force that reached San Diego on the *Cyane* on July 29, 1846. The leader, John Charles Frémont, received a fine stallion from Bandini, a gift signifying the ultimate in friendship, according to the Mexican code.

After a year of United States control, the disillusioned don wrote his son-in-law Abel Stearns: "We are in a much worse state than before. There is no government, no order, no security. Thus one sees in the towns nothing but drunkeness, gaming, sloth and public manhandling of the opposite sex . . ."

Bandini invested his store profits in a copper mine on his Baja California property. Unstable Mexican politics caused uncertainty and unnecessary expense. "Sell the mine," Stearns advised. But Bandini still saw a glimmer of promise. Next came the Gold Rush of '49. Like nearly everyone else, his mine workers hightailed it north.

I will capitalize on this gold fever, Bandini thought, and built a hotel for miners trudging across on the Gila Trail and any other travelers who happened by. The hotel operated in the red. Stearns bailed him out for the borrowed start-up money. "Get into something more reliable," the son-in-law urged at a time when Bandini owed him $34,000. But the proud old gentleman persisted despite failing health.

History writer Helen Wagner summed up matters: "Thus during the 1850s Juan Bandini was to suffer the bufferings of misfortune created by the war and the Gold Rush, Indians and outlaws, filibusters and, most deadly of all, the constantly changing political situation in Mexico . . ."

Topping things off, a wind storm damaged the hotel. A promissory note signed for another son-in-law came back to haunt him even as his health deteriorated further. He died in 1859.

William Heath Davis, who experienced setbacks himself when his New Town became known as "Davis' Folly," said of the don, "He was a man of decided ability and fine character."

The gentleman just should have quit while he was ahead.

Cave Johnson Couts:
The contradictory colonel

I n the sort of scene Hollywood later would usurp, Cave Johnson Couts and Juan Mendoza walked slowly toward each other near San Diego's Old Town Plaza. Couts, carrying a piece of cloth, cast it aside when they came within firing range, revealing his shotgun. Mendoza, spying it, whirled in an attempt to escape, but instead caught the full force from both barrels. The blast sent him reeling into a pile of grass where he died within seconds.

"Not guilty" was the verdict for Couts in 1866. His testimony persuaded the jury that Mendoza, who once worked as his major-domo, or foreman, had threatened to kill him after being fired. The jurors probably recalled Mendoza's reputation for lawbreaking in the Sonora area or the insulting challenges he leveled at his ex-employer in San Diego saloons when Couts was out of town.

A year earlier Couts had won a dismissal of an indictment for the murder of a squatter on his ranch northeast of today's Oceanside. The reason: the district attorney had not posted his bond of office. A decade before that Couts won an acquittal of charges of beating an Indian boy, and his attorney earned a dismissal of another Indian-beating charge because, he said, one juror was an alien. The Indian died.

T hese verdicts epitomize frontier justice in the tumultuous quarter century Couts spent in the San Diego area. He also served in ways to dispense it. In 1852 he became Grand Jury foreman in the case of "Yankee Jim," a six-foot, three-inch tall French Canadian whose most serious crimes included stealing a

During an 1846–49 hitch in the Army's First Dragoons, Lt. Cave Johnson Couts kept a journal that earned him a favorable place among the chroniclers of the West.

rowboat, which later was found abandoned. It was a time of violence, thievery and drunkenness, and the culprit became a scapegoat. The Grand Jury declared his crime a capital offense. Although justice may not have favored the natives or derelicts like Yankee Jim, it was at least swift. He was found guilty and hanged 31 days later. Earlier Couts served a brief term as a San Diego County judge. John Bigler, inaugurated as governor in 1852, appointed him a colonel and aide-de-camp. The honorary title of colonel stuck.

But his main claim to a niche in western history comes from a perceptive, often pithy journal he wrote during a march from Monterrey, a village in the north central section of Mexico, to Los Angeles. A lieutenant in the United States Army First Dragoons, Couts jotted down the sights, sounds and smells experienced with almost five-hundred men on the Gila Trail, a scorching and barren way made even more devastating by the command of Major Lawrence P. Graham, an alcoholic who stayed drunk most of the time. The year 1848 saw a frenzied dash northward by experienced miners from Sonora. Couts wrote:

"No corn, provisions scarce, men all deserting and going to the gold mines! Everybody crazy on the subject . . . Naked and shirt-tailed Indians and Mexicans or Californians, go and return in 15 or 20 days with over a pound of pure gold each, per day, and say 'they had bad luck and left.' "

It was less than a year after the United States victory in the war with Mexico. Couts' descriptions of life and customs in settlements along the trail acquired importance as the Gold Rush horde permanently altered the scene. His graphic description of the dragoons day-by-day progress and mishaps also delights historians. The Tennessee native, described as a southern gentleman willing to duel for a point of honor, regarded a lie as blasphemous. His fellow officers liked his geniality and fondness for jokes.

Couts transferred to the San Diego area and stayed at the home of Don Juan Bandini whose daughter Ysidora he married in 1851 when he was thirty. Among her wedding presents she received a 2,219-acre ranch from her brother-in-law Abel Stearns of Los Angeles. Six months later Couts resigned his commission.

Even before the marriage he and Bandini had joined forces on mule and horse trading deals. Before the year ended Couts converted a store into the Colorado House, complete with rooms, saloon and restaurant plus space for billiards and monte bank. The threat of an Indian uprising, led by Antonio Garra, aroused fears in a vulnerable San Diego. Couts was chosen second in command of a volunteer company, but the attack never materialized because of bickering among the tribes.

Next he served as an Indian sub-agent. The Army's bossy meddling in what Couts felt were state matters caused his resignation. It also drove him toward his wife's wedding present, Guajome Rancho, northeast of present-day Oceanside, which he developed from scratch into a "paradise," as one of his contemporaries saw it.

First he hauled in some boards and chopped down poles for a crude lean-to next to a spring he dug. He enlisted help from

Army dragoons were armed cavalrymen who dressed like this in the late 1850s. Many men from Couts' unit deserted when they heard of gold discoveries.

three-hundred Indians who dug adobe, formed it into bricks and set them in the sun to dry. Couts designed the structures, trained the brightest Indians as foremen who in turn trained the army of workers. They built a twenty room hacienda in four wings, some with walls four feet thick, around an eighty-by-ninety-foot patio complete with fountain. Workers hauled in lengthy timber from miles away. They built a small chapel for a live-in padre. He instructed ten Couts children who arrived on almost an annual basis. Even a small on-site store enabled the workers to buy goods.

Income from the sale of cattle paid for the project and for the addition of two nearby ranchos. The family fortune seemed assured until droughts, cattle thieves, squatters, sheep ranchers and fluctuating demand extracted their due. A "no-fence" law that required ranchers rather than farmers to protect farm crops virtually bankrupted Couts.

The colonel died two years later, in 1874, but not before he had insured his place in history by passing his Army journal to Hubert H. Bancroft, the San Francisco book store owner who turned historian.

A man who forsaw the day when crops, irrigated with Colorado River water, would grow on desert soil, Ephraim Morse also used his vision and energy for nearly 55 years, helping San Diego cope with challenges and capitalize on its opportunities.

Ephraim Morse:
The pious public servant

A ny member of a club, association or committee knows an
Ephraim W. Morse—but he's a man called George. As in,
"Aw, let George do it."

Morse did it all, or at least it must have seemed that way, after
settling in San Diego at the age of twenty-seven in 1850, six months
before California became a state. The town boasted a population of
about six-hundred and fifty people. First he opened a general store
with Levi Slack, his erstwhile gold hunting partner in the Yuba
River region. It seemed fitting they named their sideline venture, a
small rooming and boarding house, The Boston House, since they
hailed from Amesbury, Massachusetts.

A year and a half later Morse sailed back and married a home-
town sweetheart, Lydia Grey, but the honeymoon ended abruptly.
Indians killed his partner Slack near Warner's Hot Springs northeast of San Diego, and Morse hurried back to take charge of the
store. Lydia made the trip on her own. She died in 1856, soon after
their son was born.

In the years that followed, Morse served anywhere from a few
months to twelve years as deputy sheriff, associate judge, board of
supervisors member, board of trade secretary, a chamber of commerce organizer and treasurer of the San Diego Free Reading
Room Association, He also operated a store, sometimes solo,
sometimes with a partner. He tried ranching and farming on a
Palomar spread of one hundred acres, but found he preferred the

company of people over cattle and chickens. He became involved in the first bank, dabbled in real estate and helped launch a flume company that would carry water into San Diego.

Indoctrinated by a no-nonsense New England religious upbringing, Morse was modest yet enterprising, conscientious but often heavily in debt to vendors, a public servant who believed God helps those who help themselves. When Alonzo E. Horton arrived in San Diego in 1867, Morse wore a deputy sheriff's badge. He stood nearby when Horton observed, "The city did not lay right." Morse asked, "Where do you think the city ought to be?" and Horton replied, "Right down there by the wharf. Is there any land there for sale?"

After Morse said yes and that it could be bought at public auction, Horton pursued the proper steps, including the election of three trustees—one of whom was Morse. Morse showed Horton around the county and they became friends in the process. They bolstered each other's enthusiasm for the city's prospects. At the time of the auction, Morse loaned the visitor $123.22 as part of the bid for what soon would become "Horton's Addition."

One catalytic agent in the lives of both men was the railroad. They dreamed of an eastern link. Morse had helped organize the San Diego & Gila Southern Pacific Railroad in 1854, hoping for a line connecting any railroad from the East. Two ex-generals—William S. Rosecrans and John C. Frémont—were among the men planning or pretending a railroad link. The dream did not come completely true until 1885 and even then the eastern connection proved tenuous.

Morse submitted a resolution to the Board of Trustees in 1868 that three-hundred and twenty acres of land be set aside for a city park. The land's value could not have exceeded twenty-five dollars at the prevailing scale, but Morse's act proved his greatest legacy. The parcel of land eventually would blossom into Balboa Park.

As a young man back in Massachusetts, Morse taught school and helped on the family farm until the discovery of gold in California. He and ninety-nine other fortune hunters banded together in an unusual group.

Each member invested three-hundred dollars. With the combined total of $30,000 they bought the *Lenore* and loaded the ship with goods and supplies that could be sold or used by the company. The members agreed in their constitution "Not to engage in gambling by which money might be gained or lost, nor use any intoxicating liquors, unless prescribed by a physician, all under the penalty of a fine." They also agreed no labor would be performed on the Sabbath, "except work of necessity and mercy."

On February 4, 1849 the *Lenore* left port and docked in San Francisco Bay exactly six months later. That's when Levi Slack and Morse paired up for a frequently hot, fruitless five-month gold-panning regimen. With their remaining cash they bought merchandise and a pre-fabricated building, shipped them to San Diego and opened their store near today's G Street and Kettner Boulevard.

Morse chaired the school board during a ruckus about school teacher Mary Chase Walker. She was seen at lunch with a black woman. A high ratio of San Diego's residents favored the views of the South, so a vocal portion of her students' parents demanded her ouster. She resigned. Soon afterward Morse proposed and they married and spent thirty-three harmonious years together.

Morse died in 1906 after more than a half-century as an innovative businessman, farmer and civic-minded citizen who always seemed available when others decided, "Let George do it."

Parents made their children boycott school after Mary Chase Walker lunched with a black woman in 1866. She quit, then wed the school board chairman.

Mary Chase Walker:
The outspoken teacher

The place: San Diego
The time: July 5, 1865
The observer: Mary Chase Walker
"Of all the dilapidated, miserable-looking places I have ever seen, this was the worst."

This first impression, influenced perhaps by a bout of seasickness on the voyage from San Francisco, summed up the sorry state of San Diego's Old Town. "The buildings were nearly all adobe, one story in height, with no chimneys," she wrote in her journal. "Some of the roofs were covered with tiles and some with earth."

By society's reckoning she was far beyond the marriageable age, having reached her mid-thirties, although her trim figure and pleasant countenance brought admiring glances. San Diego struck her as an "altogether dreary, sunblasted point of departure for nowhere," a place where "crude mud houses infested with vermin crowd around a barren square in disorder."

The next spring she met a black woman, an attendant on the sidewheeler from San Francisco, who had helped make the passage a bit more bearable. Mary Walker invited her to lunch. After they were seated at the Franklin House, some diners stormed out. Others stared with contempt. Within a few days, school enrollment plunged from thirty-six to fifteen.

"We demand some action," parents told the school board

trustees. Dr. D. B. Hoffman hedged. Certainly no laws had been broken, but the board could not allow the expense of operating a half empty school room, he maintained. Robert D. Israel took an opposing view. "I'll be damned if I wouldn't take that school money and throw it in the bay as please those copperheads," he told chairman Ephraim Morse. (A "copperhead" was a Confederate sympathizer in the Civil War, which had ended May 26, 1865.) "You may do as you please, but I will never consent to her dismissal," Israel said.

Historian William Smythe said Morse, who had lost his wife ten years earlier, ended up as the "diplomatist." A former teacher

Thanks to a donation of lumber by Joseph Russ, the school named in his honor was built in 1882 and looked like this in 1887. It was an improvement on the Mason Street School where Walker taught so briefly a generation earlier.

himself, Morse had taken a liking to this spunky, outspoken woman. Thus Mary Chase Walker resigned as the Mason Street School teacher, but agreed to a different proposal. She and Ephraim Morse married on December 20, 1866 and enjoyed thirty-three years together.

Like her husband, she came from New England where she had earned four-hundred dollars a year teaching school. In San Francisco, when five dozen teachers with seniority over her ignored the San Diego job opening, Mary Walker signed up. She didn't have much choice; her cash on hand was nearly gone. She concluded two-hundred a year beat starving or going on the dole.

San Diego's rough and ready scene shocked her. The residents used coarse language. Drunks abounded. Justice often proved capricious. Some men shot first and asked questions later.

Her students, most of them of Spanish or mixed parentage, thinned out noticeably when bull fights, fiestas and other celebrations occurred. The more she learned about the ways of the Spanish and Mexican settlers, the more she enjoyed their customs, art and traditions. She even fell in love with San Diego, despite that terrible first impression.

In the years that followed her short-lived teaching career Mrs. Morse spent her spare time helping the needy. She energetically worked for the suffragette movement and celebrated on October 13, 1911 when San Diego women by a slender margin finally won the right to vote.

George W. Marston:
Prudent patron of the parks

===

When George Marston turned ninety, San Diego leaders honored him as the city's Number One citizen. No doubt about it, they said, George deserved the kudos.

This man hadn't just talked about parks, city planning and business ethics. He gave generously of money and time. He paid his department store employees above-scale, set up self-improvement courses for them and arranged musical programs in the store, brightening the day for customers.

During his birthday salute, city fathers and business leaders paid tribute with heartfelt sincerity. But time passes. People perceive the actions taken and begin comparing them with what might have been. They ask, "What if . . . ?" and that's a question even the living find difficult to answer. Consequently, Marston from this distance of time and perspective appears too wary, even prissy.

Born in tiny Ft. Atkinson, Wisconsin, in 1850, young George grew up in the yin and yang influences of a mother convinced by a religious conversion that life's purpose was a search for forgiviness of one's sinful nature and a father, George P. Marston, whose tolerant Unitarian views allowed room for enjoyment of God's gifts. Harriett Marston's strict Congregationalist mind-set dominated the house, however. The result? A puritannical atmosphere for George and his younger sisters Mary and Lilla.

When George was twenty years old his father for health reasons brought the family West. The young man came imbued with strait-laced moral views, yet tolerant about principles of others. His father had instilled in him a regard for the out-of-doors. Boyhood friends had kindled fishing, swimming and boating interests. He first worked as a clerk in the new Horton House Hotel, switched to clerking for mercantile stores, then joined with a series of partners in operating a general store, a field his father cultivated after giving up farming. By 1878, with money borrowed from his father, the young man opened his own store at Fifth and D, which later became Broadway. Ten dollars and fifty cents came in on opening day. The business struggled along and sales rose after a move to Fifth and F in 1882. Marston's prudent, hard-working bent helped the department store weather the flood of 1884, the dizzying real estate market boom and bust of the mid-Eighties and the drought years of the Nineties.

His move in 1896 to Fifth and C caused some head-shaking, but soon people saw that Marston had correctly anticipated the flow of downtown business dollars. Another shrewd move brought top-of-the-line soft goods and merchandise for appreciative upper class buyers. By the turn of the century the store employed one-hundred employees.

"A great store is more than a shop; it is a kind of institution, serving the community not only in business, but in civic affairs," he would say on the occasion of his store's fiftieth anniversary. From the outset, he was a leading example of the concerned businessman. Marston and his first partner set up a reading room in a vacant store next door. He quenched blazes as a volunteer fireman. He sparked the founding of the YMCA and served on its board sixty-two years and as president twenty-two years.

On buying trips to New York he saw landscape architect Samuel Parsons' park achievements. Marston put up $10,000 so Parsons could beautify San Diego's City Park (later renamed Balboa Park). Marston spent an additional $30,000 on its landscaping and improvements from 1902 to 1909. While he was a member of the state and county parks and beaches association, it acquired almost 500,000 acres of open space. He hired the highly regarded John Nolen who developed a well conceived city plan, except that, as critics later noted, it offered no improvements for the crowded

His upscale department store paid dividends for George Marston. A big share of them he gave to beautify San Diego, but he overlooked basic needs of people, some believe.

Mexican and Chinese sections. The plan won little support among the working class; its members wanted jobs.

Marston ended up buying the initial property for Presidio Park, hired Nolen again for the landscaping and organized the San Diego Historical Society, which helped preserve this crucial aspect of the city's Spanish heritage. "It is as important to us as Plymouth Rock on the East Coast," Marston maintained.

A jobs-vs.-appearance issue surfaced during the two times Marston ran for mayor. He promised lofty beautification and development programs. Despite support from the business community, the *San Diego Union* and the *Tribune* and from civic leaders, he lost to a no-holds-barred campaigner, Louis Wilde, who won labor's support with a "smokestacks versus geraniums" platform. Marston's daughter Mary, in a biography of her father, said, "He did not enjoy a good fight."

On July 16, 1929, the one-hundredth and sixtieth anniversary of Father Junipero Serra's arrival and the beginnings of California's first settlement by the Spaniards, the Presidio Park's Serra Museum, designed by William Templeton Johnson, was dedicated. This, too, Marston donated.

According to Gregg R. Hennessey, former San Diego Historical Society Research Archives administrator, Marston's formative years saw a flowering of Social Gospel — an avenue to salvation by way of responsible actions helping the needy. But the focus on moral regeneration ignored concrete steps such as improved housing, medical care and legal protection, Hennessey said in *The Journal of San Diego History.*

The chink in Marston's philanthropic armor was in giving merely lip service to freedom of speech, equal rights and labor reforms while devoting money and effort on parks and city planning, Hennessey said. Marston gave generously, for example, to the Chinese Mission. Nothing on record, however, indicates he argued with his Progressive Party's successful campaign for exclusionary laws against the Japanese.

How would Marston, the well-intentioned philanthropist, be remembered today if he had enjoyed a good fight? One imagines him being to San Diego what Hiram Johnson was, in his prime, to California — a man contributing government reforms and courageous direction.

Two of Marston's favorite projects. Balboa Park, left, and the Serra Museum in Presidio Park, are among the best examples of his gifts to San Diego citizens and visitors.

Dr. Harry M. Wegeforth:
The determined animal lover

For one interlude in the life of Harry M. Wegeforth his passion for animals cooled down a few degrees. Animals had first lured him to the circus, but the skills of the wire walkers intrigued him even more. At the age of eleven or so he volunteered as a backup performer. He tried out on the high wire the next year. After two more years of backyard practice he signed on and left Baltimore for a tour with the Barnum & Bailey Circus. An older brother got the assignment of tracking him down and bringing him back.

It's noteworthy he was even missed. Harry's father, Conrad Wegeforth, had six sons by his first two wives and five sons and two daughters by Harry's mother. Perhaps a family of this size is what qualified Harry to launch his own circus at the age of nine. He displayed stuffed bears, tigers and elephants. With Harry as ringmaster the neighborhood children probably could even hear them growling and trumpeting. Once two live ducks showed up for a performance. The cop patrolling the beat returned them to a nearby poultry shop; no arrests were reported.

When the weather permitted, young Harry caught crabs in the bay and returned home from the woods with snakes, frogs and an occasional turtle—all of which joined his backyard menagerie. Preoccupied with the pets, he barely squeaked by with his grades until midway in high school when he buckled down.

A touch of tuberculosis interupted plans for college. His doctor advised a trip to the high country and lots of outdoor life. So for four years Harry punched cattle in Colorado until he recovered his health.

He taught anatomy and worked in a drug store, helping pay for his University of Maryland tuition. In 1908, his M. D. certificate packed in the suitcase, he headed for Seattle. Next he set up his practice in San Diego in an office at today's Fifth and Broadway and quickly attracted patients. His glowing letters also attracted his sister Emma and brothers Paul and Arthur, also M.D.s.

As he prospered, Dr. Wegeforth acquired a new Overland and he married Rachel Granger in 1913. The newlyweds headed East in the car for their honeymoon. Two tires blew out on a rocky back country road before they could even reach the county line. The doctor hired an Indian who hitched his mules to the car and towed it to Mesa Grande. The couple consoled themselves with having a new home to which they could return, but discovered it had flooded because of a broken water pipe. The doctor's reaction? He dropped the suitcases and dashed for the dozen or so Japanese fantail fish in the pond that had flooded.

In 1915 the Panama-California Exposition scored a smashing success but the doctor squirmed about the makeshift arrangements for a display of live animals. He's reported to have exclaimed to brother Paul, "Wouldn't it be wonderful if we had a zoo." He put a notice in the newspaper, asking for support. Two other doctors and the Stevens brothers offered help. The creation of the San Diego Zoological Society became the first step in forming a zoo many people today regard as the world's finest.

Neil Morgan, the doctor's collaborator on the book *It Began with a Roar*, said, "He defied politicians. He browbeat reluctant voters. He wooed wealthy donors . . . He powdered elephants white, tossed calomel into the mouths of angry lions, and stuffed pythons with sausage from meat grinders."

Through all this, Dr. Wegeforth avoided publicity, often sneaked off when scheduled to be on the speakers' platform. For the dedication of the Wegeforth Bowl, an amphitheater where visitors learn about the zoo's residents, some friends ordered a plaque inscribed with warm sentiments about the doctor. Discomfited by the whole affair, he said, "Well, it's nice. But you could have bought an animal with the money."

The wealthy financier John D. Spreckels warned, "Watch out for this Wegeforth. If you're a patient you get your tonsils or appendix out. But if you're working on the zoo, you get cut off at the pockets."

It took fifteen years, but the zoo eventually escaped the proddings and nitpickings of politicians, thanks largely to its founder. The proposal for a non-partisan municipal commission went on

Dr. Harry Wegeforth loved cars almost as much as animals. His zeal for the live creatures helped San Diego build one of the world's biggest and best zoos.

the ballot and passed. Later, voters endorsed a tax on themselves —
two cents per one-hundred dollar valuation — for the zoo's upkeep.
Three times earlier they'd voted for it, but each time it was turned
down on technicalities.

Behind-the-scenes coaching by Dr. Wegeforth led many young
San Diego people into career fields ranging from veterinary
medicine to anthropology. Said Dr. Charles Schroeder: "He
planted the seed. We did his bidding without further interference.
He knew how to pull the most out of everyone who would help, and
you felt good about it . . . The world has known no more stubborn
or determined man."

For the quarter century Dr. Wegeforth captained the zoo's policies and operations, he cajoled money and work out of the city's
citizens of all persuasions. When funds evaporated in 1917, he
staged a big event for Marines and Navy sailors, and charged ten
cents admission — none of which the Zoological Society board knew
about before hand, let alone authorized. It worked. His hobby of
photography helped too. On all his journeys, he focused on zoos of
other states and nations. He also brought back turtles, his favorite
of all the zoo's animals.

Edward H. Davis:
Friend of the Indians

His neighbors, the Mesa Grande Indians, had made him a ceremonial chief, so other tribes visited by Edward H. Davis included him in their ceremonies. When his hosts offered food, Davis politely dined first and asked questions later. As a result he frequently learned that the tasty dish he had just eaten consisted of fried caterpillars or dog meat.

The food, the arduous travels, the hardships agreed with this talented artist, photographer and artifact collector. He lived until the age of eighty-nine, after journeying to San Diego early in 1885, hoping the climate would cure his Bright's disease.

Davis helped survey the water flume route, drafted plans for houses and worked for the company constructing the Hotel del Coronado out on the peninsula. In the midst of these jobs he dashed back to New York, married his fiancée Anna May Wills and brought her West.

The year 1885 also brought resumption of railroad service to San Diego. In the real estate boom that followed, Davis parlayed a $2,500 investment — half of it borrowed from his father — into a

$27,000 return. Most of the other speculators ended up broke when the bust arrived in the spring of 1888.

Davis bought three-hundred and twenty acres on Mesa Grande, sixty miles northeast of the city near Lake Henshaw. Then he invited his brother Irving to part from the Brooklyn, New York, homestead. Ed Davis' wife gave birth to their son Harvey. Next, Anna's mother and uncle joined the clan. At first everyone shared a small cabin with a lean-to on the side. "The only redeeming feature," Davis declared, was a large rock fireplace.

The Mesa Grande Indians, who also were called the Northern Diegueños, fascinated him. They became his lifelong friends and initiated him as a chief in 1907.

His collection of pottery, utensils, tools and other items quickly outgrew the family ranch house, requiring an adobe "museum" in back. Davis had taken art courses after graduating from high school and impressed his new friends by drawing them in their regalia. He took up photography as another way of preserving what he could see was a disappearing way of life.

Between expeditions he raised cattle, experimented with the soil to improve fruit trees, kept rain charts, served a year as deputy county assessor and another year as a justice of the peace.

In 1915 a representative of the Museum of the American Indian came from New York, checking on stories about the California collector. The visitor bought practically everything in the adobe hut, providing Davis with enough money to build Powan ("Place of Rest") Lodge on the mesa. It served as a showcase for the Indians' pottery and basket making skills, which had almost faded before Davis encouraged their revival.

The next year, George Heye, the millionaire who had founded the New York museum, called on Davis and hired him as a collector. This propelled Davis even farther afield until more than two dozen tribes in the United States and Mexico were visited over the years by the friendly, curious man with the camera, according to Charles and Elena Quinn, authors of *Edward H. Davis*.

In all his travels he never experienced problems with rattlesnakes. He killed scores of them for the protection of others. But he feared the scorpions, especially Mexico's deadly variety. His visit with the Seris on their Gulf of California island took courage. Stories of their cannabilistic rites caused almost everyone to detour

Yellow Sky, a desert Indian, became a guest of San Diego area Indians in his later years. Shown here with Ed Davis, he never slept in a bed, bathed, wore shoes, rode a horse or worked in a lifetime that spanned a century.

around the island. Not Davis. The Seris like him so much they made him a medicine man.

Before visiting a tribe, Davis checked first with the local trader, then offered to buy items at the going price. Thus the Indians and traders felt they had been treated fairly. Many tribe members sought the collector for advice and arbitration.

What began as a hobby became an almost full time occupation. In later years, after slowing down a bit, he recalled, "Those trips were the joy of my life; the freedom, the exhiliration of sleeping under the stars . . . the great unfenced open spaces."

His passion for collecting artifacts plus his drawings and photos reveal much about the Indians of the Southwest. Edward H. Davis also established bonds of trust and respect with his friends at a time when Indians were often held in contempt and persecuted.

The ocean was his oyster

The joys of San Diego and a honeymoon. What more could a young man ask?

Well, one other thing, at least for William E. Ritter. He needed some time at Point Loma. The reefs offshore sheltered the blind goby, a fish he needed for a project under way at the University of California in Berkeley.

His bride, the former Mary E. Bennett of Fresno, could appreciate his passion for research. As an M. D., she knew lowly paid university biology instructors must take advantage of study opportunities such as the San Diego area coastline offered in rich profusion in 1891.

The newlyweds struck up an acquaintance with two other doctors—Fred and Charlotte Baker. They lived in Roseville on the Point Loma promontory. With their help, William and Mary Ritter would ultimately leave an imprint on the San Diego area for all the world to see.

The next summer, William Ritter and a few students set up a tent lab in Pacific Grove, next to Monterey, for one of the earliest marine biology research efforts on the coast. UC, after some arm twisting by the enthused Ritter, appropriated two-hundred dollars for the project. The research results paved the way for more labs in the following summers.

Fred Baker in his spare time had gathered one of the finest sea

An oceanography institute director faced one drawback, William Ritter found: administrative chores left little time for digs like this on La Jolla's beach.

shell collections in the West, so he could appreciate Ritter's mission. The physician began touting the San Diego area as the perfect spot for a permanent lab. His zeal inspired the San Diego Chamber of Commerce. It set up a Marine Laboratory Committee for fund raising and Dr. Baker buttonholed civic leaders for donations.

A pledge of five-hundred dollars came from a "wealthy rancher," who turned out to be E. W. Scripps, head of a newspaper publishing empire, who directed the business from a Miramar home. Scripps and his half-sister Ellen Browning Scripps, impressed by the low-keyed, genial Ritter and possibly influenced by E. W.'s sister Virginia, became the big financial backers for today's Scripps Institution of Oceanography in La Jolla. At times E. W.'s support wavered. He once pulled out when it appeared the institute had overreached itself on construction of the lab, but rejoined the board within a year.

The Hotel del Coronado helped on Ritter's San Diego start in 1903. Elisha Babcock, the man who originated the hotel, had sold his interest to John D. Spreckels, but remained as manager. Babcock let the first batch of students use the beach house and a small launch. Ritter worried—unnecessarily, as it turned out—that the hotel's diversions would distract his young team.

Two years later the institute acquired a five-acre La Jolla site. The Ritters barely got settled when E. W. Scripps had a brainstorm. With shrewd prescience, he convinced the institute's board that it should buy a one-hundred and seventy acre parcel— the site it occupies today. The price: $1,000 at a public auction.

Ritter became the director in 1909. His challenges, in addition to dealing with the unpredictable Scripps, included keeping tabs on the work of a growing number of staff members, encouraging them, settling their differences, searching for funds from the state legislature and private donors, giving lectures and writing.

During the early years, cattle meandered into the area. Ritter even got stuck at times for mouse sitting. He had authorized the institute's first non-marine research project in 1913. It required a large number of mice and everyone took turns checking on them when the scientist in charge took off. Ritter's biggest challenge, however, came in accepting the limits on research he personally performed because of administrative demands.

William Emerson Ritter grew up in Wisconsin, toughened by the chores on the family farm. He worked to pay his way through State Normal College in Oshkosh. His experience on the debating team later proved helpful in front of students, prospective donors and the public. Tutoring services helped pay his way at Harvard University where he obtained his masters and doctorate.

Some of the eight books he wrote express the views of a philosophical biologist who sees unity in nature and the parallels between natural history and the social sciences.

He retired as the Scripps Institution of Oceanography director in 1923 and returned to Berkeley after successfully making the La Jolla research center a a mecca for scientists the world over.

——— COLOR LINE CASE ———

Anderson Obtains Judgment, but the Case Will Be Appealed

Edward Anderson, colored, obtained a judgment of $150 against John C. Fisher in Justice Bryan's court yesterday. Anderson, who was refused a seat in the orchestra circle of Fisher opera house on account of his color, sued for damages, bringing his claim originally against the Pacific Mutual Life Insurance company, owner of the opera house. This complaint was afterward dismissed, as it was found that Mr. Fisher was the sole lessee of the opera house.

The case was on trial yesterday, and the testimony showed that the tickets for the performance were purchased at noon by a colored man, and that when Anderson and his wife appeared that evening the doorkeeper took up the tickets but refused to give them a s̶ ̶ ̶ ̶'̶a̶i̶m̶e̶d̶ ̶ ̶ ̶ ̶ ̶ ̶. ticke̶ se̶

offered to allow Anderson and his wife to stand up in the balcony, but they demanded their tickets or their money. Then they were referred to Manager Fisher who plainly told them that colored people were not allowed in the orchestra circle, at the same time refunding their money, which Anderson accepted.

Judge Ryan, ruling under the new civil rights law, as passed by the last legislature, said he had no alternative but to give judgment for the plaintiff. The new law is very sweeping, and renders any keeper of an inn, restaurant, hotel, theater, bath house, skating rink, or other public place liable to damages for refusing to grant equal rights to all comers, regardless of color or ra̶c̶ The damages may be recover̶e̶d̶ ̶ ̶ ̶ ̶t̶i̶o̶n̶ brought for ̶h̶a̶t̶ ̶ ̶ ̶ ̶ ̶o̶u̶n̶t̶

Edward and Mary Anderson:
Temporary victors in a time of bias

Courage.

This characteristic must be ascribed to Edward and Mary Anderson, based on their decision to protest their treatment at the Fisher Opera House in 1897. As the accompanying *San Diego Union* article suggests, the California legislature and the United States Congress were enacting laws that guaranteed blacks their rights as citizens. But as the Andersons discovered it was one thing having a law on the books and quite another thing seeing it in force when the citizens in control believed people of a different hue should be kept in their place.

The Anderson's one-hundred and fifty dollar judgment stood as the first of its kind in the county, but they never collected. The opera

IXL Laundry, one of four businesses operated by Edward Anderson, right, produced income for entertainment such as the Fisher Opera House provided.

house won on an appeal. This surprised no one in a city that thirty years earlier had been described as the "worst copperhead hole" in the state, and where discrimination against minorities still persisted.

Segregation also continued, laws or no laws. Blacks lived mainly in the southeast side of the city. They worshipped in their own churches. And by and large they worked at menial jobs. San Diego's strong southern ties and pro-slavery adherents had been influential factors almost from the day of its incorporation in 1850, but the same type of "Jim Crow" treatment prevailed in cities throughout California.

Edward Anderson owned and operated the IXL Laundry from 1897 to 1909. During part of this time he also owned a garbage collection service, a Coronado hog farm and a San Diego mortuary still doing business in 1987, according to *Black Pioneers in San Diego: 1880-1920*, a twenty-four page booklet by Gail Madyun and Larry Malone. Anderson was an exception. Most of the three-hundred or so blacks in the city in 1900 worked as porters, servants, cooks, bootblacks, janitors and unskilled laborers. Others came and went as longshoremen and sea hands. The Andersons probably were among the two dozen black families who owned their own homes then. Joseph A. Steward was likely another member of this home owners' group. He was the first black person admitted to the San Diego Bar. That occurred in 1891.

Treatment of blacks proved less onerous than Indians and Chinese experienced in the San Diego area. For one reason, the blacks were few in number. The 1890 census showed two-hundred and eighty-nine black people in town out of a total population of 16,159. Ten years earlier, only three blacks were counted.

An 1850 law prohibited blacks, Indians and Chinese from testifying against white people in civil and criminal cases. The ban was lifted for blacks thirteen years later. California in its early years held the dubious distinction among the states of placing perhaps the most legal stumbling blocks in the way of black children's education. An 1874 law suit brought a ruling that children of African descent would be educated in separate schools, but if a local school board didn't provide the facility, black children could join the white school. In practice, however, black parents usually sued their local board before it complied. In 1880, California lawmakers passed a measure prohibiting school segregation.

Blacks won the right to vote in 1869 with the ratification of the Fifteenth Amendment to the Constitution, which stated the "right of citizens of the United States to vote shall not be denied or abridged in the United States, or any State, on account of race, color or previous condition of servitude."

From 1850 until 1948 blacks could not intermarry with whites. In some cases prior to 1870, blacks were not even allowed to farm.

The church became a central aspect of life for most San Diego blacks. The Second Baptist Church and Bethel A.M.E. Church evolved by 1888 and the Mt. Zion Baptist Church at the turn of the century. Edward Anderson belonged to Fidelity Lodge No. 10 of the Masons, which was made up of black men. It's likely he belonged to one of the four republican clubs because practically all blacks belonged to the party after the Civil War.

The black heritage in the San Diego area includes the last Mexican governor, Pio Pico, and his brother Andrés. Their grandmother's name appeared on a 1790 census as a "mulatta." A United States sailor, John Brown, went A.W.O.L. in 1804 while his ship the *O'Cain* was in port, making him the first United States black to trod San Diego soil. Nathaniel Harrison became the county's first permanent black resident, according to *Black Pioneers in San Diego*. A Tennessee slave, he arrived in 1848 and built a cabin part way up Palomar Mountain where he raised livestock for more than fifty years and became widely known.

Fred Coleman discovered gold near Julian in 1869. This started a stampede by land swindlers, claim jumpers and prospectors. Today's Julian Hotel got its start in 1887 when Albert and Margaret Robinson built and operated the structure which bore the family name for twenty-seven years. It is Southern California's oldest continuously operated hotel.

M.O. Medina:
Leader of the fishing pack

"**M**. O., you are crazy."
That's how the commercial fishermen reacted when Manuel O. Medina at the age of twenty took the plunge by ordering a fifty-one-foot vessel powered by a thirty-five horsepower engine. The year was 1914. Vessels used by the one-dozen Portugese fishermen then in San Diego were only slightly larger than Medina's old eight-horsepower *Beauty*. He, however, had watched Julius Zolezzi and some of the other Italians returning with large catches in their faster, bigger vessels and realized big was not only better, it was essential to survival.

A friend, Manuel Madruga, built the new boat in the yard of his Old Town home next to a brewery. In those days a fisherman could obtain financial help from the canners who accepted part of a catch as their installment payment. This plus the money for the sale of the *Beauty* got Medina started. He named the new craft *Pacifico*.

Medina, like his transplanted countrymen, came from the isle of Pico, Azores. He had arrived in San Diego late in 1912 after working a year on a Half Moon Bay ranch. This provided a stake of one-hundred dollars; he borrowed a hundred and fifty more and bought the *Beauty* with his cousin. They trolled for barracuda, bonita and yellowtail from February through April. The catch — cut, dried and bundled — was sacked and sold through Point Loma fishermen acting as agents. They paid off when the fish reached San Francisco one month afterward. The young partners barely broke

A leader in this Feast of the Holy Ghost Parade in 1915 and in the Portugese community, M. O. Medina, left, served on this holiday as a flag bearer.

even until Medina said they should experiment by fishing for rock cod in the off months. Later he declared, "The rock cod fishing's what saved me." With the *Pacifico* under his feet, he boosted his catches and even added an Ensenada-San Diego lobster run. After two years in the Army, he talked with A. J. Steele, owner of a packing company bearing his name, who decided a market existed for canned tuna. Steele said, "I'm willing to pay you a hundred dollars a ton for any tuna you catch and if you don't have any luck whatsoever I'll pay your expenses for the trip." Two weeks later Medina returned from the waters off San Benito Island with eleven tons iced down—the first sizable catch of what would one day become a yearly multi-million dollar tuna fishing industry for San Diego.

Two more successful tuna trips followed, but the *Pacifico* developed engine problems midway in 1920. They proved a blessing in disguise.

Medina borrowed a sixty-foot vessel that the Union Fish Company had picked up after her owner ran afoul of legal problems. Before weighing anchor, a friend, Joe Rogers, handed Medina a barbless hook with feathers, which he had acquired from a Japanese skipper. Medina gave it a try—and got the workout of his life. "I was pulling fish in so fast I kept the whole crew busy handling them," he said. He returned with thirty-two tons of tuna, a catch big enough to merit a newspaper story.

The barbless hook, baited with a "squid" of feathers and the belly skin of a fish, became standard for the tuna fishermen. Crew members stood atop gratings suspended over the sides or the stern, sometimes up to their waists in water. When leaping tuna signaled that a school was nearby, the "chummer" dipped live bait from tanks and scattered enough around to lure the fish closer. When they went for the bait flicking just above the water, the fisherman simultaneously heaved the catch up and swung it aboard—all in one smooth flowing motion.

It was risky. A man pulled overboard stood little chance of emerging from the frenetic, closely packed school of tuna. If he did, the sharks, attracted by fish blood spilling from the scuppers, presented another dangerous guantlet. One mistake and the barbless hook could open a long gash in a fisherman close by.

When a two-hundred and fifty pound tuna hit a line it took three

Two or three men teamed together for the biggest catches in the risky, physicallly demanding job aboard a tuna vessel in an industry that began about 1907.

men reacting as one to save the pole—and sometimes the man holding it. If the pole began flopping in the midst of a school, the fish were scared off. The really big ones had to be heaved overboard; the maximum legal limit was one-hundred and fifty pounds. Medina kept moving upscale. He asked Madruga to build the *Oceana*, a sixty-six-footer with a ninety-horsepower diesel engine. This became San Diego's first diesel-powered tuna vessel. The cost in 1924: $15,500. A year later, after selling this vessel for the same amount he paid for it, he commissioned the *Atlantic* for a cost of $55,000, then continued to enlarge and improve additional vessels as the years went by. Catches of 1,200 tons became possible. Trips to Central and South America were commonplace in vessels with 600-horsepower engines.

He never lost a vessel. Two that he operated did go aground off Baja California; one at Sacramento Reef and the other at Akreojos. In both instances he maueuvered the vessels off without outside help and saved the fish loads.

A fearless captain who knew and loved the sea, M. O. Medina seemed to stand taller than his five-foot, six-inch size. He was a long-time leader in his church and a president of the Port Brotherhood. He died on March 14, 1986.

Ah Quin:
A Chinese Horatio Alger

If **Ah Quin were alive today,** you could picture him in the company of Lee Iacocca, Tom Peters and other best-selling authors of the business success genre. The title of Ah Quin's book might well be *How to Achieve the American Dream*. For achieve it he did against odds far greater than Iacocca or Peters confronted.

Men and a few women of all nationalities stormed into California during the 1849 Gold Rush. The number of Chinese in the state reached about 75,000 by 1880. To say they were unwelcome is an understatement.

Two things about the Chinese disturbed a lot of people: they worked hard and they did so for low wages. What's more, most of the hard-earned wages went back to families in China, where nine out of ten of her emigrants planned one day to return. As the irreverent columnist Herbert Lockwood once pointed out, their un-American traits of sobriety, silence and frugality proved downright upsetting.

As early as 1852 California enacted a miner's tax strictly for the industrious Chinese. The state's constitution in 1878 halted them from entering California, prohibited them from owning real estate and from working for the government. The United States followed suit four years later with an Exclusion Act that stopped Chinese immigration entirely. An American who married a Chinese back in those days automatically lost his or her citizenship.

In Los Angeles a mob lynched nineteen Chinese in 1871. San

Franciscans rioted against the Chinese in 1877 and the day afterward a San Diego crowd plotted a riot of its own, but sheriff Joseph
Coyne's well-armed Committee on Public Safety defused the plan
by parading downtown with a show of their artillery. According to
historian Hubert Howe Bancroft, "In the annals of our Coast there
is no fouler blot than the outrage perpetrated at various times and
places upon the Chinese."

How could one man buck this tide of prejudice?
Ah Quin had picked up a smattering of English in a Canton,
China, mission school. He improved it after arriving in San
Francisco in 1868 and working as a cook in Seattle and Alaskan
fishing camps. An uncle in Santa Barbara taught him the basics of
running a store. When Ah Quin first visited San Diego in 1878,
department store mogul George Marston and Presbyterian
Church minister G. W. Camp met him and later suggested he settle
in the city.

Two years later at the age of twenty-seven Ah Quin arrived. He
cut off his queue—the Chinese man's traditional long braid of hair.
He also quickly found opportunity as the labor contractor for the
California Southern Railroad, which needed construction crews
for its National City-San Bernardino line. Ah Quin scoured Los
Angeles and San Francisco, then established ties in China, round-
ing up laborers for work that paid up to one dollar and seventy-five
cents a day. He supplied as many as eight-hundred workers their
rice, potato and fish meals from his store on Fifth. He also served as
paymaster, confidant and counselor, all of which brought in one
dollar per day per man gross.

At one point the San Diego Chamber of Commerce asked
businessmen to close their stores for a Horton House rally supporting the Exclusion Act. This was in 1882 when the Chinese population in the city had reached about 1,000. By the following year, the
number plummeted to three-hundred. Some cities passed ordinances requiring that Chinese people remain indoors after sunset.

Enterprising Chinese started San Diego's fishing industry, and
Ah Quin sold them supplies. The entrepreneurs built junks out of
redwood for fishing runs south to Cabo San Lucas and north to
Monterey. Some fishermen, working off of sampans, monopolized

Most Chinese immigrants were "sojourners"—those who planned to return. But Ah Quin settled in San Diego and raised one of the earliest Chinese clans.

the abalone catch. It proved doubly valuable because of the demand in China for abalone shells for jewelry making. Fish profits evaporated, however, after the passage of a law in 1888. It prohibited people who were not United States citizens—and this included all Chinese—from reentering the country if they ever went outside the three-mile territorial limit.

The treatment of Chinese in San Diego was kinder than in San Francisco or Los Angeles due, perhaps, to their smaller number or, more likely, to enlightened people like George Marston who led in the start of the Chinese Mission School.

Ah Quin leased and bought—when it was legal—parcels of land as far north as Los Angeles and ran vegetable gardens on shares with the farmers, then sold the produce in his store. When tourmaline, a crystalline silicote, was discovered in Julian, he bought in

Eighteen junks operated out of San Diego Bay in the mid-1880s. Their Chinese owners bought hooks, lines and other items at Ah Quin's store.

on the mining action, influenced, no doubt, by the knowledge of the fondness for the gemstone by the Empress of China. She craved only the pink ones.

Once established in San Diego, Ah Quin revisited San Francisco and returned with a bride, Sue Leong. They raised a dozen children. As the years rolled along, he became a wealthy man, a respected business leader, a spokesman for the Chinese and often an interpreter for them. He died at the age of sixty-six after a motorcycle hit him in an intersection.

His son George and grandson Joe carried on some of the business enterprises, and descendants of Ah Quin today are San Diego area leaders in business, civic matters and culture, beneficiaries of the spirit of San Diego's Chinese Horatio Alger.

Katherine Tingley:
Colorful star of theosophy

With dramatic flair Katherine Tingley directed a halt for her retinue of five influential Americans on what was billed as a world crusade in 1896.

They had successfully created a European branch of the Theosophical Society. They won favorable reviews with Brotherhood suppers for the poor in England and with membership drives in France and Holland. And the "Purple Mother," an affectionate title based on her fondness for the color, amazed her group by, sight unseen, divining the spot in Killarney where they discovered a green rock, sought as a cornerstone at Point Loma, the proposed site of the society's new school.

So the crusaders took a break at Interlake, Switzerland, near the ruins of an ancient building. "Perhaps we could find another cornerstone in the rubble," she suggested. In the exciting prospect of a fresh discovery, however, a cable from the society's vice president cast a pall. It said: "Impossible to purchase place you name; it is owned by the U.S. government."

Tingley, for one of the few decision-making times in her life, was speechless. She had selected the San Diego promontory without so much as a visit. It had been described to her nearly ten years earlier by explorer and Civil War General John C. Frémont only weeks before he died. Her intuition convinced her the site would be perfect, not only for a school but also for a utopian community.

Now with the disappointing cable message on a table before her, Tingley stood silent. Precisely on cue, Gottfried de Purucker made his entrance. A practicing theosophist, American by birth and a former San Diego resident, he introduced himself. Upon discover-

Principles of Karma and reincarnation drew followers to Katherine Tingley's society. Her charisma held sway over a membership that reached 100,000 world wide.

ing the problem, he quickly drew the curled finger shape of the land protecting the city's bay and explained that the U.S. owned only the fingernail portion. She quickly cabled back: "The site of the school is exactly where I said; the U.S. government land is south of it. Make inquiries and buy quickly."

No one announced why one-hundred and thirty-two acres of Point Loma land were being purchased. A *San Diego Tribune* headline early in 1897 asked, "What Does It Mean?" Some residents guessed a posh gambling resort would follow. Others imagined a steamship terminal. After the school plan was announced, nearly 1,000 of the citizenry joined in the laying of the cornerstone — one of local origin; the Killarney rock had been delayed in reaching California's shore.

So San Diego became the home first of the Raja Yoga (Royal Union) School in 1900, then the Theosophical Society headquarters. Tingley rewrote the group's constitution, giving herself complete lifetime control, and changed its name to The Universal Brotherhood and Theosophical Society. Forty buildings, three of them topped by green-or amethyst-colored domes, sprang up. One story has it that as visitors drove in, a bugler hidden behind an Egyptian gateway would step forth and herald their arrival.

Theosophy, usually translated as *divine wisdom*, at first puzzled then outraged San Diego clergymen. Belief in reincarnation, the occult and the esoteric proved too much for all but the Unitarians to accept. "In the name of Christianity and innate sense, San Diegans ought to protest this bold affrontery [sic]," concluded the Reverend Clarence True Wilson, pastor of the First Methodist Church. Tingley attracted a packed Fisher Opera House for her rebuttal, but there's no evidence this caused people to change their views. The big changes came as a result of factions within the movement trying to upstage one another and the closing of United States Theosophy Society lodges as Point Loma drained away their money and their best brains.

General Harrison Gray Otis, opinionated publisher of the *Los Angeles Times*, which frequently disparaged San Diego, discovered at Point Loma what he regarded as an easy target. In 1901 the paper headlined a story, "Outrages at Point Loma." The subheading added: "Women and Children Starved and Treated Like Convicts." The story said, "Gross immoralities were practiced by the disciples of spookism." Tingley's libel suit found five attorneys for each side arguing over claims that her dog Spot was the reincarnation of her ex-husband, and the flimsiness of her followers' robes was indecent. The jury took three hours to award her $7,500. More importantly, it taught editors throughout the country responsible reporting saves money.

Dr. George F. Mohn, who, with his wife, was among the first to pay $500 to become Point Loma residents, contributed $300,000 to the cause. Mrs. Mohn finally took a dim view of his generosity and sued Tingley for alienation of affections. The jury decided Mrs. Mohn deserved $75,000 back. Another ex-follower complained, "I wore long gowns and ridiculous hats in her presence and tried to take part in the foolish ceremonies, with some belief that they might have a meaning. But I knew it meant that pretty soon we would have to crawl into Mrs. Tingley's presence on all fours."

Critics like these failed to deter her, though. She organized campaigns against war, capital punishment and vivesection. The transforming power of Raja Yoga education would reform the world, she believed, as schools were started in Cuba, Sweden, San Diego, San Francisco and Roseville. She told an Amsterdam conference, "I love to think of our boys brought up this way, in our senates, working as law-makers, diplomats. I grow young thinking of them. And it is not so far ahead. Some day our race will be one race, one Universal Brotherhood, one government, one language, and we shall enjoy eternal peace."

Born in 1847 in Newberry, Massachusetts, she was sent by her Puritan parents to a convent, but quickly dropped out and married a printer. They called it quits after two months. Virtually nothing is known about Tingley's next decade except one member of her inner theosophy circle suggested that she had joined a traveling stock company, as reported in Emmett A. Greenwalt's well balanced book, *The Point Loma Community in California 1897-1942.*

"Certainly she gave evidence of stage experience when in later years she introduced dramatic productions among theosophists," according to Greenwalt. In 1887 she met Theosophical Society

Raja Yoga (Royal Union) calesthenics class takes a halt in 1905 on a Point Loma site that had grown by then to 500 acres. "The Homestead," right, housed some of the members; others built their own homes.

leader William Quan Judge and influenced him with her talents as a maternalistic medium. After his death nine years later, she commanded center stage of the disorganized society.

She entranced wealthy backers like Albert G. Spalding of sports equipment fame and impressed her inner circle with her canny decisions. The Purple Mother, however, lacked an occult guideline on finances. The organization's spending invariably exceeded income. Her death in 1929, coupled with the country's economic collapse, gradually lowered the curtain on the Point Loma experiment in 1942.

"The greatest strength of Point Loma sprang from its uniting faith," Greenwalt observed. It helped introduce Oriental thought to the United States and made significant contributions in the field of education, he said.

While a Nebraska newspaper editor, William Smythe focused on irrigation improvements as the best way of coping with droughts and restoring arid lands.

William E. Smythe:
Little Landers' social engineer

The majority of people who filled San Diego's Garrick Theatre that night of July 28, 1908 ranged from the middle aged on up to retirees. Most of them were city folks, too, which seemed a bit odd because the speaker, William E. Smyth, talked about farming.

He proposed that a man and his wife with a little land, in cooperation with other small farm operators close by, could earn a living while enjoying a wholesome social life without the hassles of the city.

Times were tough. Banks had closed because of the Panic of 1907. People lost their jobs. Farmers went bankrupt. Smythe passionately believed his remedy could help, not just in San Diego but across the nation.

"What is wanted is a form of country life that shall bring the people reasonably close to the great towns, both for market and social advantages; that shall give them near and numerous neighbors; that shall permit . . . a quick, rich, up-to-date social and intellectual life — full, elevating, satisfying," he said.

He spoke with authority as an experienced journalist, a self-educated leader in farm irrigation methods and as the author of one of San Diego's best written history books. Smythe described the success of people growing gardens on vacant town lots. He cited how the Mormons transformed barren Utah lands. He said the

"Little Landers" colony he proposed was not a philanthropy; it was a business venture.

Despite his rousing platform oratory, only a dozen families signed up for the suburban utopia he envisioned. Each family agreed to pay from $350 to $550 for a farming acre, depending on its location, and $250 for a 50-by-120-foot building lot close to the proposed community center. The $250 included a stake in the irrigation system and utilities. People who paid cash received a discount.

He challenged the men. This enterprise gave each one of them a chance to become "a man with initiative . . . an independent, self-employing man. To his trees, his plants and his vines he gives the ineffable touch of love. He is the spiritual man of the soil."

L ittle Landers began on 120 acres of land 14 miles south of San Diego on the site of today's San Ysidro. Some speculators jumped on the band-wagon as the colony grew and neglected their agreements. The others, however, pitched in with enthusiasm. Hard work and good weather, along with ample water that wells provided, produced harvest surpluses, which they bartered for coffee, clothes and tools. One member with a horse and buggy rounded up vegetables and fruit each day and sold them in town.

Within four years one-hundred and sixteen families called themselves Little Landers. There had been difficult times and turnover, but now a new downtown co-op market on Sixth Street displayed their crops. Similar suburban colonies grew in Alameda County, the San Fernando Valley and near San Jose and Palo Alto.

At Little Landers a spiritual emphasis included church gatherings and hymn sings in the clubhouse where evening school sessions, poetry readings and lectures also took place. It became a life based, not on social revolution, but on brotherly love under Smythe's guidance.

As the years passed, though, many of the older city-bred farmers learned that a single acre, even when intensively farmed, didn't produce a comfortable income year after year. Then the big flood of January 1916 buried more than half of the colony's land under sand and debris. Two women died in a rescue mishap. World War 1

Little Landers, Smythe's brainchild, had attracted 116 families in 1913, four years after it started in today's San Ysidro area. A family could live off of one irrigated acre with hard work, intensive farming and cooperative neighbors, he said.

sapped the colony's strength. Smythe's death in 1922 brought the closing chapter in the utopian experiment.

Smythe's legacy doesn't hinge on utopian engineering alone. In addition to *The History of San Diego* he wrote *Constructive Democracy: The Economics of a Square Deal.* This second book consists of speeches Smythe made during a campaign for congressman from California's Eighth District. He lost in a close race to Republican M. J. Daniels, who had served as a captain in the Civil War. Ironically, Republican President Theodore Roosevelt espoused an irrigation and reclamation platform built on the ideas of Smythe.

William Ellsworth Smythe was born on Christmas Eve in 1861 in Worcester, Massachusetts. The ancestors of his mother, Abbie Bailey Smythe, went back to the Puritans. Her husband, William Augustus Somerset Smythe, was a well-to-do shoe manufacturer.

Young William experienced a pleasant childhood. One of his

idols, newspaper editor Horace Greeley, wielded a strong influence; William became editor of his high school newspaper, edited the *Kearney (Nebraska) Enterprise* in 1888, then moved up a year later to the *Omaha Bee* just before a serious drought threatened the Great Plains. He launched a series of irrigation editorials and stories and became so knowledgeable farmers elected him head of the newly formed National Irrigation Congress. He founded and edited *Irrigation Age*, gave talks around the country and his articles appeared in leading magazines.

His **influence on irrigation** proved so great he belongs on a pedestal alongside Luther Burbank, John Muir and Father Junipero Serra, said George W. James in *Heroes of California.*

During the depression that caused a full house at the Garrick Theatre in 1908, Smythe said, "A little land and a living, surely, is better than a desperate struggle and wealth, possibly." Today about one-hundred utopian colonies exist in the United States, suggesting the Little Landers' spirit still lives.

255

INDEX

Acapulco, 79, 80, 82
Advertising
 Coronado, blitz, 184
 "Nuvida Water," 103, 104
 Outdoor, Ida Bailey, 95
Adler & Sullivan, architects, 17
Aerial Experiment Assn., 30
"Aeroplane(s)," 23, 26, 27, 28
Agua Caliente Race Track, 52
Airmail, 31, 38
Alabama, 41
Allen, Capt. James, Mormon Bn., 110
Allen, John, Mormon Bn. 110
Allesandro, *Ramona* hero, 7
Alta (Upper) Calif.,58, 59, 60, 76, 82, 126
 (see also California)
Alvarado, Juan Bautista, 9
Alvarado, Pedro, 75
Ameche, Don, in film *Ramona*, 10
America, 20, 22, 69 (see also United
 States)
American
 Bar Assn., 146
 Bayreuth, 20
 Legion, 19
 River, 84
 Riviera, 174
 West, 83
American(s), 3,21, 84, 87, 88, 89, 91
Ames, John J., editor, 43
Anderson, Edward, Mary, 231-4
Architecture
 African 17
 English, 17
 Mission, 17
 Queen Anne, 12, *13*
 Spanish Colonial, 17, 140
 Victorian, 12, *13*
 Villa Montezuma, 11, 12, *13, 14*
Arguello, Sandieguito, 26
Arizona, 122, 123
Arkansas, 123
Army (see U. S. Army)
Arnold, Gen. Henry "Hap," 35
Asbury College, 74
Ashley, Wm. H., fur trader, 84
Associated Press, 48
Atchinson, Topeka & Santa Fe R. R., 178,
 179, 187

Atlantic Ocean, 31, 75, 82
Austria, 21
Aviation Hall of Fame, 39
Aztecs, 75

Babcock. Elisha, 182-6, 229
Bailey, Ida, madam, 95-98
Baja Calif., 61, 82, 115
Baker, Drs. Fred, Charlotte, 227
Balboa Park, 18, 19, 39, 52, 137-41
 149, 206
Baldwin, E. J. "Lucky," 123
Balloonists, 26, 30, 31
Bancroft, Geo., Secty. of Navy, 92
Bancroft, Hubert H., historian, 175, 191,
 203, 242
Bandini, Juan, 93, 195-8, 202
Bandini, Ysidora, 202
Bank of America, 100
Bank of Calif., 165
Baptist Church, 72
Baptists, 173
Barnum & Bailey Circus, 219
Barry, Capt., Fitch's ally, 158
Barstow, 188
Bartlett, John, Boundry Com., 168
Bartlette, Mrs., re V. Scripps, 48
Barton, deputy chief, 72
Beale, Lt. Edward F., 131
Bean, Roy, first jailee, 162
Bear Flag Revolt settlers, 92
Behan, Johnny, lawman, 123
Bell, Alexander Graham, 30
Benchley, Belle, J. 152-5
Bennett, Mary E., nee Ritter, 227
Benson, alias for Hatfields, 52
Berkeley, 138, 230, 227
Bible, 84
Bigler, Gov. John, 201
Binney, Fred, realtor
Birmingham, U.S.S., ship, 28
Blaisdelles, Solon, 138
"Black Friday," 177
Black, Jeremiah, attny. gen., 191
Blacks, 231-234
Blaylock, Celia, Wyatt Earp's wife, 123

AUTHORS CITED

ORDER FORM

Order Fulfillment Dept., California Profiles Publications, P.O. Box 23727, Pleasant Hill, CA 94523:

Please send _____ copies of *San Diego Originals* in the ☐ hardbound ☐ softbound edition. Enclosed is my check or money order for $ _____ .

(Hardbound cost is $19.95 plus $1.50 shipping. Softbound is $12.95 plus $1.50 shipping. For two or more copies sent to same address, add 25 cents each. California residents add 6% sales tax. For air mail shipment, add $2.50 plus 50 cents for each additional book.)

Send to:

Name _____

Address _____

City _____ State _____ ZIP _____

Name _____

Address _____

City _____ State _____ ZIP _____

Name _____

Address _____

City _____ State _____ ZIP _____